MW00578616

Victory is Mine!

BARBARA JOHNSON

Fleming H. Revell
A Division of Baker Book House Co
Grand Rapids, Michigan 49516

Victory is Mine!

BARBARA JOHNSON

Fleming H. Revell
A Division of Baker Book House Co.
Grand Rapids, Michigan 49516

VICTORY IS MINE

© 1996: Christian Art, P O Box 1599, Vereeniging, 1930, South Africa

Designed by: Christian Art

ISBN 0-8007-7159-1

Printed in Hong Kong

JANUARY

JANUARY 1

YOUR FIRST DAY OF RECOVERY

*"Rid yourselves of all the offenses
you have committed, and get a new
heart and a new spirit ... "*
Ezekiel 18:31

You can begin your recovery today. You don't have to wait another minute. This can be "New Year's Day" for your Year of Recovery. I won't pretend that recovery is easy or quick. It is neither. It's hard work and commitment, but it does happen. God is waiting to help you begin your first day of recovery. Take Him up on His offer.

JANUARY 2

A SPOTLESS TRACK

*Command them to do good, to be rich
in good deeds, and to be generous and
willing to share. In this way they will
lay up treasure for themselves as a firm
foundation for the coming age ...*
1 Timothy 6:18, 19

*T*he new year lies before you like a
spotless track of snow. Be careful how
you tread it for every mark will show.

JANUARY 3

A GOOD LAUGH

A happy heart makes the face cheerful,
but heartache crushes the spirit.
Proverbs 15:13

A resolution for the New Year:
Learn to laugh. A good laugh
is better than medicine.

JANUARY 4

KIND THINGS

*And we urge you, brothers, warn those
who are idle, encourage the timid, help
the weak, be patient with everyone.*
1 Thessalonians 5:14

A resolution for the New Year:
Learn the art of saying kind
and encouraging things.

JANUARY 5

A NEW YEAR'S RESOLUTION

*A cheerful look brings joy to the heart, and good
news gives health to the bones.*
Proverbs 15:30

A resolution for the New Year: Learn to
greet your friends with a smile. They
carry too many frowns in their own
hearts to be bothered with any of yours.

JANUARY 6

BIBLICAL RESOLUTIONS

*I press on toward the goal to win the
prize for which God has called me
heavenward in Christ Jesus.*
Philippians 3:14

Some biblical resolutions for the
coming year: I will, like Paul, forget
those things which are behind and press
forward. I will, like David, lift up mine
eyes unto the hills from whence comes
help. I will, like Abraham, trust implic-
itly in God. I will, like Job, be patient
under all circumstances.

JANUARY 7

TODAY IS HERE

Whatever your hand finds to do,
do it with all your might ...
Ecclesiastes 9:10

*D*ream not too much of
what you'll do tomorrow,
How well you'll work another year;
Tomorrow's chance you
do not need to borrow —
Today is here.

JANUARY 8

A FRESH START

*Consider him who endured such
opposition from sinful men, so that you
will not grow weary and lose heart.*
Hebrews 12:3

If you fail in one place, that doesn't
make you a failure. Sure, we all fall, but
it's how long you stay down that counts.
Get up, begin again, and you will know
the joy of a fresh start with Jesus.

JANUARY 9

ONLY ONE ME

*I praise you because I am fearfully
and wonderfully made; your works
are wonderful, I know that full well.*
Psalm 139:14

I celebrate me!
I am worth everything. I am unique. In
the whole world there is only one me.
There is only one person with my talents, my experiences, and my gifts.

JANUARY 10

THE NOW

*If we confess our sins, he is faithful
and just and will forgive us our sins
and purify us from all unrighteousness.*
1 John 1:9

It doesn't matter my age, color, or
whether I was loved as a child or not.
Let all that go. That belongs to the past.
I belong to the now! It doesn't matter
where I have been, or mistakes I've
made, or hurts I have had. I am for-
given. I am accepted. I'm okay. I am
loved in spite of everything.

JANUARY 11

A FRESH DAY

He who was seated on the throne said, "I am making everything new ... Write this down, for these words are trustworthy and true."
Revelation 21:5

*T*oday can be a fresh day, a new beginning. This earth suit will be gone one day, traded in for a robe of white — until then I have today to enjoy!

JANUARY 12

FROM WHERE WE ARE

Do not conform any longer to the pattern of this world, but be transformed by the renewing of your mind. Then you will be able to test and approve what God's will is ...
Romans 12:2

We can't really live our whole lives over again, but we can make progress from where we are right now to where God wants us to be. The only time it's too late to change our lives is when we reach heaven – God's eternal today.

JANUARY 13

MINUTES OF GOLD

[Make] the most of every opportunity ...
but understand what the Lord's will is.
Ephesians 5:16, 17

Minutes of Gold.
Two or three minutes –
two or three hours,
What do they mean in this life of ours?
A minute may dry a little lad's tears,
An hour sweep aside
the trouble of years.
Minutes of my time may bring to an end
Hopelessness somewhere,
and bring me a friend.

(Author Unknown)

JANUARY 14

WE WILL WIN THE GAME

*... let us run with perseverance the race marked
out for us. Let us fix our eyes on Jesus, the
author and perfecter of our faith ...*
Hebrews 12:1, 2

God doesn't promise us that we'll
be leading at the half, but He did
promise we would win the game.

JANUARY 15

A LONG-TERM INVESTMENT

But I trust in you, O LORD ...
My times are in your hands ...
Psalm 31:14, 15

You can recover and gain confidence in
your children by remembering that
loving your child is a long-term invest-
ment, not a short-term loan. Love is
worth the time it takes to grow, and
growing a child is not a quick process.

JANUARY 16

A DIFFERENT PERSPECTIVE

Now we see but a poor reflection as in a mirror; then we shall see face to face. Now I know in part; then I shall know fully ...
1 Corinthians 13:12

*I*t's amazing how one's attitude about something can change with a different perspective.

JANUARY 17

GOD USES OUR FAILURES

Therefore, if anyone is in Christ, he is a new creation; the old has gone, the new has come!
2 Corinthians 5:17

God uses even our failures to make better people of us. Jesus saw men, not as they were, but as they were to become, filled with His Spirit and dedicated to His work. There's nothing wrong with failure. There's plenty wrong with giving up.

GOD HAS PLANNED THE FUTURE

When I called, you answered me;
you made me bold and stouthearted.
Psalm 138:3

*G*od will bring healing, patience, and comfort when you don't think you can survive another day. Don't grieve over the past; rejoice that God has already planned the future.

NEVER TOO OLD TO LEARN

*He who heeds discipline shows the
way to life, but whoever ignores
correction leads others astray.*
Proverbs 10:17

Most of us are long past the time
of going to school, studying, and
taking tests. Most of us are even past
preparing our children for school and
tests. But no matter what our ages,
we are never too old to learn.

WHAT I DO TODAY

*"But seek first his kingdom and his
righteousness, and all these things
will be given to you as well."*
Matthew 6:33

*T*his is the beginning of a new day. God
has given me this day to use as I will. I
can waste it – or use it for good, but
what I do today is important, because I
am exchanging a day of my life for it!

JANUARY 21

THE PAST IS OVER

*Brothers, I do not consider myself yet
to have taken hold of it. But one thing
I do: Forgetting what is behind and
straining toward what is ahead ...*
Philippians 3:13

No matter what has happened in the
past, that is over. No matter how much
you wish the past had been different,
you cannot change what has already
happened. Don't mourn over what is
done; rejoice that there is still a future!

JANUARY 22

REACH OUT

Do not be anxious about anything, but in everything, by prayer and petition, with thanksgiving, present your requests to God. And the peace of God, which transcends all understanding, will guard your hearts and your minds in Christ Jesus.
Philippians 4:6, 7

God is present and ready to help you right where you are. Reach out in a simple prayer to Jesus and feel Him now take your hand. With His hand and power at work in your life, you, too, can have your tears turned into joy, your night into day, your pain into gain, your failures into successes, your scars into stars, and your tragedy into triumph.

JANUARY 23

USE TODAY WISELY

"Therefore do not worry about tomorrow, for tomorrow will worry about itself. Each day has enough trouble of its own."
Matthew 6:34

Yesterday is a canceled check, tomorrow is a promissory note, but today is cash! Use it wisely.

JANUARY 24

EMBRACE THE FUTURE

*" ... This day is sacred to our Lord.
Do not grieve, for the joy of
the LORD is your strength."*
Nehemia 8:10

*H*ow we look at life can determine
where we will find joy in our exercise
of beginning again. This is what I
wish for you: that you will find joy in
sorrow, let go of the past, and embrace
the future God has given you today,
and work on using today wisely.

GOD'S GRACE FOR TOMORROW

*Those who know your name will
trust in you, for you, LORD, have
never forsaken those who seek you.*
Psalm 9:10

Life is not over just because you have experienced a devastating blow. Begin again today, and trust God's forgiveness to take care of yesterday, and His grace to take care of tomorrow.

NO TRAGEDY LASTS FOREVER

*Yet he did not waver through unbelief
regarding the promise of God, but
was strengthened in his faith ...*
Romans 4:20

While life isn't always the way we want it, no tragedy lasts forever. Recovery and survival are in reach. We can walk together, patiently enduring the sorrow and depression as we grow up from the valley onto the mountaintop. Sorrow may flood you repeatedly, but each time you will survive, stronger and happier than before.

JANUARY 27

THE FINAL REWARD

*I have fought the good fight, I have
finished the race, I have kept the faith.*
2 Timothy 4:7

*T*here are days when I wonder what is so
great about hanging in there. For what?
And then I remember the final reward:
standing before the Lord and knowing I
have fought a good fight, have kept the
faith, and have finished the course.

JANUARY 28

ACCEPT WHAT YOU HAVE

*(G)ive thanks in all circumstances, for
this is God's will for you in Christ Jesus.*
1 Thessalonians 5:18

Nothing is perfect, nothing will be
exactly right, but we can enjoy and
appreciate what we have, not what
we wish we had. We need to learn
to accept what God has for us.

RAINBOWS FROM TEARS

*Let the peace of Christ rule in
your hearts ... And be thankful.*
Colossians 3:15

*T*hrough the wetness of your tears,
your own sorrow will begin to glisten.
You can go from the pits, where it is
black, to beige, and then to rainbows,
which come from tears in our lives.
Your constant habit of being a joy
collector will be your therapy.

JANUARY 30

COLLECT LIFTERS

The prospect of the righteous is joy, but the hopes of the wicked come to nothing.
Proverbs 10:28

Collect all the things in life which are lifters, not sinkers. You need encouragement and lightness. Start looking for it!

JANUARY 31

JOY IS THE PRESENCE OF GOD

> *The LORD is my shepherd, I shall
> not be in want. He makes me lie down
> in green pastures, he leads me beside
> quiet waters, he restores my soul ...*
> Psalm 23:1-3

Joy is not the absence of suffering but
the presence of God. We all go through
pain and sorrow, but the presence of
God, like a warm, comforting blanket,
can shield us and protect us, and allow
the deep inner joy to surface, even in the
most devastating circumstances.

FEBRUARY

FEBRUARY 1

MAKE THIS A LOVE MONTH

*Remember this: Whoever sows sparingly
will also reap sparingly, and whoever
sows generously will also reap generously.*
2 Corinthians 9:6

Let's concentrate on making February a
love month. Let's learn to love life and it
will love us back. What you give is what
you get. Life is like a boomerang – if you
throw it out it will come back to you.

FEBRUARY 2

SCRIPTURE'S SOFT PILLOW

*"And we know that in all things God works
for the good of those who love him, who have
been called according to his purpose."*
Romans 8:28

*"A*nd we know that all things work
together for good to them that love
God" ... (Romans 8:28 KJV). This is
Scripture's soft pillow for a tired heart!

FEBRUARY 3

GOD'S LOVE NEVER FAILS

*For I am convinced that neither death nor life,
neither angels nor demons, neither the present
nor the future, nor any powers, neither height
nor depth, nor anything else in all creation,
will be able to separate us from the love of
God that is in Christ Jesus our Lord.*
Romans 8:38, 39

*E*ven when our parental love seems all
spent and wasted, even when our best
intentions and prayers seem to have
produced children who reject us and
the Lord, God's love never fails.

GOD'S LOVE CAN HEAL HEARTS

"For God so loved the world that he gave his one and only Son, that whoever believes in him shall not perish but have eternal life."
John 3:16

God loved us so much that He sent His Son to die for us. God's love never fails, and it can heal our hurting parents' hearts as well as mend our children's rebellious hearts.

FEBRUARY 5

GOD HAS A PLAN

*... When I was woven together ... your
eyes saw my unformed body. All the
days ordained for me were written in
your book before one of them came to be.*
Psalm 139:15, 16

I am absolutely convinced that life
does not happen by chance. God has
a plan; God's plan is full of His love
for us; and God's plan will succeed!
When we are in the midst of pain it
is hard to believe that, but I know
it's true, and I've seen it work!

FEBRUARY 6

LOVE YOUR CHILD UNCONDITIONALLY!

Above all, love each other deeply, because love covers over a multitude of sins.
1 Peter 4:8

Don't forget to love your child unconditionally! He or she may pierce your heart with actions which seem to you to be designed especially to hurt you. But your job is not to judge, not to condemn, not to get revenge. Your job as a Christian and a parent is to love that child in the midst of everything!

GIVE YOUR LOVE AWAY

"Greater love has no one than this, that
he lay down his life for his friends."
John 15:13

Life's greatest joy is to give your
love away. As you allow God's love
to flow through you and you give
that love out, God will use you to
touch another person who needs
to feel the warmth of that love.

SPENDTHRIFTS IN LOVE!

*Let no debt remain outstanding, except the
continuing debt to love one another, for he who
loves his fellowman has fulfilled the law.*
Romans 13:8

It would be great if we could
all be spendthrifts and just buy
anything in sight. But we can be
spendthrifts in love! Love is the
one treasure that is multiplied by
division. It is the one gift that grows
bigger the more you take from it.

FEBRUARY 9

DWELL ON GOD'S LOVE

*Keep yourselves in God's love as you
wait for the mercy of our Lord Jesus
Christ to bring you to eternal life.*
Jude verse 21

When you have "down" days (and
we all do), and you feel that the
black pit has you again, just dwell
on God's love. How rich and full it is!
Let His love keep you and give you
rest. Just rest in God's love, which is
a shield around your hurting heart.

LOVE POURED

*... (L)ive a life of love, just as Christ
loved us and gave himself up for us as a
fragrant offering and sacrifice to God.*
Ephesians 5:2

*W*e cannot pour love on others
without spilling it on ourselves.

THE STRENGTH TO RISK LOVE

We love because he first loved us.
1 John 4:19

Don't be afraid to share your love. Don't be afraid to give your love to a wayward child. Nothing will happen to you and your love that God isn't ultimately in charge of. He will give you the strength to risk your love, and the glue if your heart breaks and needs mending.

FEBRUARY 12

A FRAGILE THING

*Praise be to the God and Father of
our Lord Jesus Christ, the Father of
compassion and the God of all comfort,
who comforts us in all our troubles ...*
2 Corinthians 1:3, 4

*T*his heart of mine is such a fragile
thing. Like fine porcelain, I could set
it on a shelf, but I tend to put it rather
in the midst of life. Thus it has been
broken a million times. Perhaps the glue
with which God mends it is stronger
that the stuff of which it is made.

(Author Unknown)

FEBRUARY 13

WARM COMPASSION

*Carry each other's burdens, and in this
way you will fulfill the law of Christ.*
Galatians 6:2

So many people are lonely today.
Every time you give someone else a
lift, you get a lift. Compassion is one
healing, uplifting gift that God gives
to each of us to use. Warm compassion
can break the chains that bind us and
transform a cold, indifferent world
into a warm, loving one.

FEBRUARY 14

PEOPLE LIKE YOU AND ME

Brothers, think of what you were when you were called. Not many ... were wise ... influential ... of noble birth.
1 Corinthians 1:26

Who does God use? He uses people like you and me. Don't let past failures hinder you. Failure is a tough teacher, but a good one. Let God's love flow through you to help those who are hurting, needing the love you can release to them.

FEBRUARY 15

LOVE IS ...

*It [love] always protects, always trusts,
always hopes, always perseveres.*
1 Corinthians 13:7

*L*ove is ...
Slow to suspect ... quick to trust. Slow
to condemn ... quick to justify. Slow to
offend ... quick to defend. Slow to
belittle ... quick to appreciate. Slow to
demand ... quick to give. Slow to pro-
voke ... quick to conciliate. Slow to
hinder ... quick to help. Slow
to resent ... quick to forgive.

LOVE IN ACTION

And now these three things remain: faith, hope and love. But the greatest of these is love.
1 Corinthians 13:13

Love's ABC's
Love Accepts, Behaves, Cheers,
Defends, Enriches, Forgives,
Grows and Helps. Love Includes,
Joins, Kneels, Listens, Motivates,
Notices, Overlooks, and Provides.
Love Quiets, Respects, Surprises,
Tries, Understands, Volunteers,
Warms, eXpects, and Yields.
Love in action breaks the code
that adds Zip to your life!

FEBRUARY 17

WILLING AND OPEN

"I am the Lord's servant," Mary answered.
Luke 1:38

God's love is expressed through other
people to us. You don't have to be a
perfect saint to be able to share love
with someone else. You don't even
have to be especially mature as a
Christian to share God's love. You
just have to be willing and open.

FEBRUARY 18

A FRAGRANT BALM

*But for you who revere my name, the
sun of righteousness will rise with healing
in its wings. And you will go out and
leap like calves released from the stall.*
Malachi 4:2

God's love is like a fragrant balm that
does double duty. When you spread
God's love balm on someone else, it
not only heals that person, but
brings healing to you as well.

FEBRUARY 19

GIVE YOUR BROKEN HEART TO GOD

*Surely he took up our infirmities
and carried our sorrows ... and
by his wounds we are healed.*
Isaiah 53:4, 5

God can heal your heart. God can rescue
you from despair and give you something to rejoice about again. It won't
happen overnight, but it will happen.
All you have to do is be willing to give
every piece of your broken heart to God.

THE GIFT OF GOD'S LOVE

*"You are the light of the world. A
city on a hill cannot be hidden."*
Matthew 5:14

Give every single little piece of your
heart to the Lord, and He will begin
the mending process. You will survive,
times will get better, and you will,
with the grace of God, be able to help
others with the gift of God's love.

FEBRUARY 21

SOME LOVE HOMEWORK

*Let no debt remain outstanding, except the
continuing debt to love one another, for he who
loves his fellowman has fulfilled the law.*
Romans 13:8

Give yourself some love homework
this month. Assign yourself the task
of loving someone you don't really
like. I don't mean that you will make
yourself her best friend, but determine
(make a decision of the will) that you
will be obedient to Christ and love
her, in spite of her shortcomings.
God will bless you for that.

THE GREATEST POWER

*Who shall separate us from the love of Christ?
Shall trouble or hardship or persecution or
famine or nakedness or danger or sword?
No, in all these things we are more than
conquerors through him who loved us.*
Romans 8:35, 37

Love unleashes the greatest
power under heaven.

I KNOW

He heals the brokenhearted and
binds up their wounds.
Psalm 147:3

I know God will help you. I know God
will heal you. I know that there is hope.
I have been there, I have been restored.

FEBRUARY 24

GOD'S FILTER OF LOVE

For Christ's love compels us ...
2 Corinthians 5:14

With God's love, you can face and go through anything! Nothing comes into the life of a Christian without first passing through God's filter of love.

FEBRUARY 25

EXPERIENCE

*God is our refuge and strength, an ever-present
help in trouble. The LORD Almighty is with
us; the God of Jacob is our fortress.*
Psalm 46:1, 7

*E*xperience is yesterday's
answer to today's problems.

PRAYER AND FAITH

*Now faith is being sure of what we hope
for and certain of what we do not see.*
Hebrews 11:1

Prayer is asking for rain and
faith is carrying the umbrella.

MANY DETOURS

*Lazy hands make a man poor, but
diligent hands bring wealth.*
Proverbs 10:4

*T*he road to success has many detours
because it is always under construction.

FEBRUARY 28

LIFE

... The race is not to the swift or the battle to the strong, nor does food come to the wise or wealth to the brilliant or favor to the learned; but time and chance happen to them all.

Ecclesiastes 9:11

Life is a bundle of little things and the string is always coming untied.

FEBRUARY 29

AN ACTION WORD

Be devoted to one another in brotherly love.
Honor one another above yourselves.
Romans 12:10

Love is an action word.
You have to show love.

MARCH

PAINFUL MEMORIES FADE

*Restore to me the joy of your salvation and
grant me a willing spirit, to sustain me.*
Psalm 51:12

*G*od removes the sting, and time does
allow us to remember the good, while
painful memories seem to fade away
like water-colored pictures in the rain.

MARCH 2

YOU ARE GOING TO MAKE IT

*May the God of hope fill you with all
joy and peace as you trust in him, so
that you may overflow with hope by
the power of the Holy Spirit.*
Romans 15:13

After the storm is over, there are bittersweet memories. After the first few
months of shock and panic, some of the
pain is drained off and healing begins.
You begin to feel better for longer
periods of time. You can go for a few
hours and not be consumed by thoughts
of your wayward child. Then, pretty
soon, you can survive a whole day
without anguish. That is when you
know you are going to make it after all!

MARCH 3

LOVE INVESTED

*"... weep for ... your children. For the time
will come when you will say, 'Blessed are
the barren women, the wombs that never
bore and the breasts that never nursed!'"*
Luke 23:28, 29

What we mothers have to recognize is
that it is all right to hurt – hurt is a
measure of the love we have invested in
someone else. There is risk involved with
love, and too often, heartache. But the
alternative is a life of gray and dullness.

MARCH 4

STEADY AND SURE

I will betroth you to me forever; I will betroth you in righteousness and justice, in love and compassion.
Hosea 2:19

Love doesn't have to be profound, or educated, or dazzling. It just has to be there, steady and sure, even in the bad times.

MARCH 5

RELY COMPLETELY ON GOD'S DIRECTION

The Sovereign LORD is my strength;
he makes my feet like the feet of a deer,
he enables me to go on the heights.
Habakkuk 3:19

When we have problems in our lives
which seem so often to have no reason,
and we lack any understanding of them,
we have to rely completely on the
lighthouse of God's direction for our
lives and the rock of Christ's salvation.

CLING TO HIM

*He [Job] replied, " ... Shall we accept good
from God, and not trouble?" In all this,
Job did not sin in what he said.*
Job 2:10

We don't have all the answers. Some
days I wonder if we have any, yet I know
that when we throw up our hands after
trying fruitlessly to make sense out of all
this, we can only cling to Him, and
know that we don't have to understand.

MARCH 7

TRUSTING HIM

*... God has said, "Never will I
leave you; never will I forsake you."*
Hebrews 13:5

Nothing comes into our lives until it first
passes through the will of God. He has
promised never to leave us or forsake us.
Trusting Him is all we can do to carry us
through the times when we flounder and
see no way ahead of us to go on.

MARCH 8

THE ROCK

*He alone is my rock and my salvation; he
is my fortress, I will never be shaken.*
Psalm 62:2

We have a lighthouse that never
moves or changes: the will of
God. And the rock that lighthouse
stands on is Jesus Christ.

MARCH 9

SOMETHING POSITIVE

*Test me, O LORD, and try me, examine
my heart and my mind ... My feet stand
on level ground; in the great assembly
I will praise the LORD.*
Psalm 26:2, 12

Grief and mourning are a necessary
part of growing through the hard
times. Through your suffering, God
will help you to recover and will give
you something positive out of it all.

THIS TOO WILL PASS

*" ... This is what the LORD, the God
of your father David, says: 'I have heard
your prayer and seen your tears ... '"*
Isaiah 38:5

*I*n the midst of your grief, just hang
on to the idea that this too will pass,
and God will use it for good.

MARCH 11

NOT TOO LONG

"Therefore I will not keep silent; I will speak out in the anguish of my spirit, I will complain in the bitterness of my soul."
Job 7:11

Determine today that you will suffer long enough to acknowledge the pain of your situation, but not so long that you get comfortable with grief.

MARCH 12

THE LIGHT OF CHRIST

*In him was life, and that life was the light
of men. The light shines in the darkness
but the darkness has not understood it.*
John 1:4, 5

The light of Christ is waiting just around
the corner, waiting for you to ask for
change and recovery. Even when we
don't think we see anything positive
in our circumstances, God's plan is
quietly unfolding behind the scenes.

MARCH 13

THAT KIND OF LOVE

*... Having loved his own who were
in the world, he now showed them
the full extent of his love.*
John 13:1

*T*he love of a parent for a child should
be a reflection of the love God has for
each of His spiritual children. That's
a love that can be hurt. That's a love
that can cause pain. That's a love that
can suffer, but can't be turned off.
That kind of love is precious.

MARCH 14

IN GOD'S CARE

*Blessed is the man who makes
the LORD his trust ...*
Psalm 40:4

Don't give up your love for your
child – put it in God's care and
trust God for the healing.

MARCH 15

MY ROCK OF REFUGE

*In you, O LORD, I have taken refuge;
let me never be put to shame; deliver me in
your righteousness. Turn your ear to me,
come quickly to my rescue; be my rock of
refuge, a strong fortress to save me. Into
your hands I commit my spirit; redeem
me, O LORD, the God of truth.*
Psalm 31:1, 2, 5

In you, O Lord, I have taken refuge; let
me never be put to shame; deliver me in
your righteousness. Turn your ear to me,
come quickly to my rescue; be my rock
of refuge, a strong fortress to save me.
Psalm 31:1, 2 NIV

A VERY PRESENT HELP

But the eyes of the LORD are on those who fear him, on those whose hope is in his unfailing love. We wait in hope for the LORD; he is our help and our shield.
Psalm 33:18, 20

You will find Him to be, just as He promised, "a very present help in time of need".

A REFUGE FOR SOMEONE ELSE

*... make every effort to add to your faith ...
godliness; and to godliness, brotherly
kindness; and to brotherly kindness, love.*
2 Peter 1:5, 6, 7

Sometimes the Lord directs us to become places of shelter and hope for others. Have you ever thought about being a refuge for someone else? Few roles are more gratifying, but in order to be a refuge for someone else, you need to be loving, compassionate, and accepting. Christians, we need each other!

SHARED SORROW

*I can do everything through him
who gives me strength. Yet it was
good of you to share in my troubles.*
Philippians 4:13, 14

There's an old Swedish proverb
which says, "Shared joy is a double
joy. Shared sorrow is half a sorrow."

MARCH 19

SHARING OUR HURT

"My command is this: Love each other as I have loved you. Greater love has no one than this, that he lay down his life for his friends."
John 15:12, 13

*F*inding a refuge ... isn't that what we are all doing? People who hurt as we hurt need a place to cry, a person to care, the security of intimate friends who will share our hurt.

TOGETHER

*As iron sharpens iron, so one
man sharpens another.*
Proverbs 27:17

You can begin your own healing by being a refuge for someone else. You can do for others what you need for yourself. Open your heart to someone else, even when you are in pain yourself. Together you can encourage each other and pray for each other.

MARCH 21

THAT PLACE OF COMFORT

*Therefore, my dear friends ... continue to
work out your salvation with fear and trem-
bling, for it is God who works in you to will
and to act according to his good purpose.*
Philippians 2:12, 13

In this process of healing and becoming,
which we are all in, let us reach out and
help others find that place of comfort,
pointing others to the one shelter of
God's care, a refuge for a wounded one.

GOD CARES

*"Come to me, all you who are weary and
burdened, and I will give you rest."*
Matthew 11:28

My gift for your March is a twofold
thought: get rid of the garbage of
bitterness that is contributing to your
depression; find the Lord's refuge,
from which you can be a refuge for
someone else. Remember, God
knows; God cares and remembers, too.

MARCH 23

TURNING IT AROUND

*"Take my yoke upon you and learn from me,
for I am gentle and humble in heart, and
you will find rest for your souls. For my
yoke is easy and my burden is light."*
Matthew 11:29, 30

As bad as anything can become, God
is that much better at turning it
around for good, happiness, and life.

THE CHOICEST COUNSELORS

He will sit as a refiner and purifier of silver; he will purify the Levites and refine them like gold and silver. Then the LORD will have men who will bring offerings in righteousness.
Malachi 3:3

You who have endured the stinging experiences are the choicest counselors God can use. Remember, others have been there, too.

MARCH 25

NO WAY

... *"Who then can be saved?" Jesus looked at them and said, "With man this is impossible, but with God all things are possible."*
Matthew 19:25, 26

*T*here is no way to silence the grief of having to mourn a loved one who has not died.

THE HARDEST TEACHER

*The crucible for silver and the furnace for gold,
but man is tested by the praise he receives.*
Proverbs 27:21

*E*xperience is the hardest kind
of teacher ... it gives you the test
first and the lesson afterwards.

ITS SONG

... *I will refine them like silver and test
them like gold. They will call on my
name and I will answer them ...*
Zechariah 13:9

The brook would lose its song
if God removed the rocks.

DRAIN THE PAIN

Command them to do good, to be rich in good deeds, and to be generous and willing to share.
1 Timothy 6:18

Secrets are to sickness as openness
is to wholeness. Drain the pain
by sharing with another.

MARCH 29

GOD'S BLANKET OF LOVE

*(A)nd to know this love that surpasses
knowledge – that you may be filled to
the measure of all the fullness of God.*
Ephesians 3:19

*T*ake God's comfort blanket of love,
wrap it snugly around you, and enjoy
the warmth and protection it offers.

STRONGER THAN EVER BEFORE

*He heals the brokenhearted
and binds up their wounds.*
Psalm 147:3

I love you and have compassion for you, for the hurt, bewilderment, and pain you are going through right now. And I love you for what God is going to do in your life, mending your broken heart, putting the pieces back together, stronger than ever before.

MARCH 31

OUR BURDENS

"Take my yoke upon you and learn from me, for I am gentle and humble in heart, and you will find rest for your souls. For my yoke is easy and my burden is light."
Matthew 11:29, 30

We cannot let our burdens paralyze our progress.

APRIL

APRIL 1

IT IS PROMISE

*... And we rejoice in the
hope of the glory of God.*
Romans 5:2

April is promises – April is a good
month. It is hope. It is promise. It is
newness ... signs of spring; couples
walking hand in hand in the park,
jumping rope, jacks, marbles, baseball,
neighbors calling across fences, house-
wives hanging out winter clothing to air.

APRIL 2

THE GREAT STIRRING

*"Consider how the lilies grow. They do
not labor or spin. Yet I tell you, not even
Solomon in all his splendor was dressed like
one of these. If that is how God clothes the
grass of the field, which is here today, and
tomorrow is thrown into the fire, how much
more will he clothe you, O you of little faith!"*
Luke 12:27, 28

April is rakes, forks, spades, and
lawn mowers on the sidewalk in front
of the hardware store. It is rain on the
weekends, mud on the kitchen floor,
and dirt and grass stains on the knees
of blue jeans. April is the great
stirring, the doorway to May.

APRIL 3

BE HAPPY

Rejoice in the Lord always.
I will say it again: Rejoice!
Philippians 4:4

This month's message to you is:
BE HAPPY! I hope you all will enjoy
the silliness which comes with April
Fools, and the hope of spring!

THE VALLEY OF DESPAIR

... we also rejoice in our sufferings, because we know that suffering produces perseverance; perseverance character and character, hope.
Romans 5:3

We all find ourselves in the valley of despair sometimes. But I believe we grow in the valley, because that's where all the fertilizer is! So learn to welcome the valley times, and see all the growth in character that comes from them.

APRIL 5

A NEAT IDEA

*"Who of you by worrying can add
a single hour to his life?"*
Matthew 6:27

I developed a neat idea someone suggested to me: "Life isn't what you want, but it's what you've got, so stick a geranium in your hat and be happy!"

THE FLOWERS OF GOD'S GRACE

*His divine power has given us
everything we need for life and godliness
through our knowledge of him who called
us by his own glory and goodness.*
2 Peter 1:3

*W*e can choose to gather to our
hearts the thorns of disappointment,
failure, loneliness, and dismay in our
present situation. Or we can gather the
flowers of God's grace, boundless love,
abiding presence, and unmatched joy.
I choose to gather the flowers.

SHARING HELPS

*A man of many companions may
come to ruin, but there is a friend
who sticks closer than a brother.*
Proverbs 18:24

*W*e have some great times of sharing
with relatives and friends. Sharing
does help drain the pain parents go
through with wayward children.

OVERFLOWING LOVE

*Your love has given me great joy and
encouragement, because you, brother,
have refreshed the hearts of the saints.*
Philemon verse 7

*T*o see anger and bitterness and hardness
disappear, to be replaced by a gentle
spirit and overflowing love, is exciting!

THE JOURNEY TO WHOLENESS

Brothers, I do not consider myself yet to have taken hold of it. But one thing I do: Forgetting what is behind and straining toward what is ahead, I press on toward the goal to win the prize for which God has called me heavenward in Christ Jesus.
Philippians 3:13, 14

We are all on the journey to wholeness. Some are farther down the road, some have stopped at resting places, and some have even detoured. But none of us have arrived!

LIFT THEM UP

*Therefore, strengthen your feeble
arms and weak knees. "Make level
paths for your feet," so that the lame
may not be disabled, but rather healed.*
Hebrews 12:12, 13

When you are low down, with arms
drooping down and bent knees,
then read Hebrews 12:12 – "Where-
fore lift up the [drooping] hands
... and the feeble knees" (KJV).

THE GARDEN OF YOUR MIND

Finally, brothers, whatever is true, whatever is noble, whatever is right, whatever is pure, whatever is lovely, whatever is admirable – if anything is excellent or praiseworthy – think about such things.

Philippians 4:8

Remember the nursery rhyme, "Mary, Mary, quite contrary, How does your garden grow?" How about the garden of your mind? You can let weeds sprout and multiply, let them choke out new life. Or, you can cultivate the garden of your mind and watch your days bloom one by one.

FAITH IS SOUL FOOD

*We always thank God for all of you,
mentioning you in our prayers. We continually
remember ... your labor prompted by love,
and your endurance inspired by hope ...*
1 Thessalonians 1:2, 3

*F*ertilizer is plant food and faith is
soul food. Without fertilizer, your
garden cannot flourish, and your
spirit cannot grow without faith.

APRIL 13

SINCERE LAUGHTER

Our mouths were filled with laughter,
our tongues with songs of joy.
Psalm 126:2

*H*e who laughs, *lasts*! So put guffaws, snickers, giggles, and titters high on your priority list. Sincere laughter is a powerful tonic for a weary, battered soul.

GOD KEEPS HIS PROMISES

*Because God wanted to make the
unchanging nature of his purpose
very clear to the heirs of what was
promised, he confirmed it with an oath.*
Hebrews 6:17

God always keeps His promises.
You will get through and you
will get back in the flow of life.

APRIL 15

A SENSE OF HUMOR

*Rejoice in the LORD and be glad, you right-
eous; sing, all you who are upright in heart!*
Psalm 32:11

*H*aving a sense of humor is what
has saved me from the pits. I still
get there, but I don't stay there.
You have to learn to develop a sturdy
ladder to climb out of the pits — one
rung at a time, probably. Laughter
and humor are the bottom rungs on
which to start the upward climb!

APRIL 16

THE SPIRIT OF FUN

*Sing, O Daughter of Zion; shout
aloud, O Israel! Be glad and
rejoice with all your heart ...*
Zephaniah 3:14

The value of fun lies in the spirit of it,
whether it is climbing windmills, or
marching in a parade, or going up on
the down escalator. Break out of your
little plastic mold and become a real
dingy person (not din-gee, but ding-ee),
even if people think you are fresh out
of a rubber room. Laughing helps.
It's like jogging on the inside.

APRIL 17

FUN THINGS

"I have told you this so that my joy may be in you and that your joy may be complete."
John 15:11

Look for ways to enjoy your day, however small or trivial. Begin to look for fun things. They are there.

APRIL 18

MARVEL

So God created man in his own image,
in the image of God he created him;
male and female he created them.
Genesis 1:27

*L*ook at people and marvel at how each
one is a unique reflection of God's
creative diversity. Look at a field of
flowers and see flowers, not weeds.

LOOK FOR FUN

*All the days of the oppressed are wretched, but
the cheerful heart has a continual feast.*
Proverbs 15:15

I have learned to find fun in unlikely
places. Fun is a mystery. You cannot
trap it like an animal; you cannot
catch it like the flu. But it comes without bidding if you are looking for it.

THE GARMENT OF JOY

*The prospect of the righteous is joy, but
the hopes of the wicked come to nothing.*
Proverbs 10:28

When life gets so heavy and you wonder
how you can cope with all the load,
learn to put on the garment of joy for
the spirit of heaviness – and fun is
included in that garment of joy.

POSTPONE NEGATIVITY

*... we take captive every thought
to make it obedient to Christ.*
2 Corinthians 10:5

Make a list of everything that is
preventing you from being happy
today. Consider postponing all nega-
tive feelings for twenty-four hours.

ONE SUCCESS EXPERIENCE

*He who works his land will have
abundant food, but the one who chases
fantasies will have his fill of poverty.*
Proverbs 28:19

Give yourself at least one success
experience today. It could be
doing exercises you hate or
completing an unpleasant task.

LOVE SEEDS

Be devoted to one another in brotherly love.
Honor one another above yourselves.
Romans 12:10

Keep sending out love messages and planting love seeds in your family.

APRIL 24

MAKING A DIFFERENCE

*Children's children are a crown to the aged,
and parents are the pride of their children.*
Proverbs 17:6

You do make a difference in
your child's life, even if he or
she is denying you right now.

LEAVE IT IN GOD'S HANDS

Do not be anxious about anything, but in everything, by prayer and petition, with thanksgiving, present your requests to God.
Philippians 4:6

How good that we can leave it in God's hands and know that He has all the answers in His time for us.

APRIL 26

GOD'S COMPASSION TOWARD THE SINNER

*(F)or all have sinned and fall short
of the glory of God, and are justified
freely by his grace through the
redemption that came by Christ Jesus.*
Romans 3:23, 24

We must always remember that
God hates sin and yet is so tender and
compassionate toward the sinner.

APRIL 27

HE PROVIDES A NET

*The LORD is my shepherd ... He makes
me lie down in green pastures, he leads me
beside quiet waters, he restores my soul ...*
Psalm 23:1-3

God will never let you sink under
your circumstances. He always provides
a net. His love always encircles you.

APRIL 28

FIND SOME WAY

*And the disciples were filled with
joy and with the Holy Spirit.*
Acts 13:52

Do whatever makes you laugh —
tasting Christmas on old pine
branches, or hibernating with old
"I Love Lucy" reruns. Find some
way to flatten out your pain.

APRIL 29

THE FULL VALUE OF JOY

*When the righteous triumph,
there is great elation ...*
Proverbs 28:12

Grief can take care of itself; but to
get the full value of joy, we must
have somebody to share it with.

THE WISH TO SCATTER JOY

*Now that you have purified yourselves
by obeying the truth so that you have
sincere love for your brothers, love one
another deeply, from the heart.*
1 Peter 1:22

There is no beautifier of complexion,
or form, or behavior, like the wish to
scatter joy and not pain around us.

MAY

MAY 1

THE WORD IS HOPE

*But Christ is faithful as a son over God's house.
And we are his house, if we hold on to our
courage and the hope of which we boast.*
Hebrews 3:6

In May, the word for you to hug
close to you is hope – because
Mother's Day always brings to mind
memories of former happy days.

MAY 2

CLEANING OUT

Have mercy on me, O God ... blot out
my transgressions. Wash away all my
iniquity and cleanse me from my sin.
Psalm 51:1, 2

May is a time for cleaning out
drawers, putting fresh paper on shelves,
dumping collections of junk we have
squirreled away. Clever housekeepers
keep an unused dust mop to shake out
the front door. Then they shake the
real one out the back door at night.

MAY 3

CLEARING AWAY COBWEBS

Search me, O God, and know my heart;
test me and know my anxious thoughts.
See if there is any offensive way in me,
and lead me in the way everlasting.
Psalm 139:23, 24

May is the month for throwing open
doors and clearing away the cobwebs.

ROOTS AND WINGS

*Fathers, do not embitter your children,
or they will become discouraged.*
Colossians 3:21

There are two things we can give
to our children. One is roots, and
the other is wings. Yes, the first
is easier to give than the last.

GIFTS TO CHERISH

*Fathers, do not exasperate your children;
instead, bring them up in the training
and instruction of the Lord.*
Ephesians 6:4

Children are not properties to own
and rule over. They are gifts to
cherish and care for. Our children
are our most important guests. They
enter into our home, ask for careful
attention, stay for a while, and then
leave to follow their own way.

LETTING GOD

*Cast all your anxiety on him
because he cares for you.*
1 Peter 5:7

We have to give our children to God and then take our hands off. It is like wrapping a package up and putting on a label, and then being able to send it, without our special directions of where to go, but letting God put the address on the label – or on that life.

BEING A MOTHER

*Love is patient, love is kind. It does not
envy, it does not boast, it is not proud.
It always protects, always trusts,
always hopes, always perseveres.*
1 Corinthians 13:4, 7

You know you are a mother when
– you have an assortment of seventeen
handmade ashtrays, and no one in
your family smokes.
– your three-year-old calls you into
the bathroom to retrieve the Star
Wars soldier out of the toilet.
– your freezer is packed with the
twenty-seven boxes of Girl Scout
cookies your daughter couldn't
sell to anybody else.

A DEEP LOVE

Love never fails.
1 Corinthians 13:8

A mother's love goes on and on,
even when her child is grown and
gone. God planted a mother's love
so deep that the roots of it go
deep and far into our hearts.

MAY 9

NOT ALONE

*Be completely humble and gentle; be patient,
bearing with one another in love.*
Ephesians 4:2

*Y*ou are not in this alone. There
are thousands of mothers trying to
make this day meaningful, so do it by
planting your love in someone else.

MAY 10

A MOTHER'S HEART

*No one has ever seen God; but ... God lives
in us and his love is made complete in us.*
1 John 4:12

Be glad you have a mother's
heart; your love is special.

A REFRESHING DAY

*[Make] the most of every opportunity
because the days are evil.*
Ephesians 5:16

Make Mother's Day a good, refreshing
day. Remember back to when Mother's
Day meant breakfast in bed, handmade
sticky "presents" from kindergarteners?
We seem to have forgotten some of
those earlier, happier days!

THE KNOT OF HOPE

*We have this hope as an anchor
for the soul, firm and secure ...*
Hebrews 6:19

We know that when we get to the end of
the rope, we tie a knot and hang on ...
but do you know what that knot at the
end of the rope is called? It is hope.
That's the possession of each Christian,
because we have a solid basis for hope.

HOPE SPRINGS ETERNAL

"(B)ut whoever drinks the water I give him will never thirst. Indeed, the water I give him will become in him a spring of water welling up to eternal life."
John 4:14

Hope springs eternal, and is held by the bedrock of God's love.

MAY 14

GET ON WITH IT

*Yet he [Abraham] did not waver
through unbelief regarding the promise
of God, but was strengthened in his
faith and gave glory to God.*
Romans 4:20

*R*emember, there is work to do,
and God will do what He promises.
We have to get on with the business
of life, not get stalled on the tracks
and run over by the train of doubts.

MAY 15

THAT LIGHT

*But Christ is faithful as a son over God's house.
And we are his house, if we hold on to our
courage and the hope of which we boast.*
Hebrews 3:6

Who can describe hope to anyone?
Hope is that light at the end of the
tunnel, when all around you is black.

JUST PLAIN HONESTY

Anyone who is among the living has hope ...
Ecclesiastes 9:4

Hope doesn't always have to be sunny.
Sometimes hope is just plain honesty.
Sometimes when we are so down that
we don't even think there is an up,
honest expression of our feeling is as
close to hope as we can get.

BECAUSE OF

*Although he was a son, he learned
obedience from what he suffered ...*
Hebrews 5:8

It is because of the suffering, the pain
and loss and separation, that we grow.

TO BECOME GOLD

*The crucible for silver and the furnace
for gold, but the LORD tests the heart.*
Proverbs 17:3

Your feelings are honest and normal —
but not forever. We are in the
furnace of pain to become gold,
not to melt away to nothing.

MAY 19

NEVER GIVE UP HOPE

*Now it is God who has ... given us the Spirit
as a deposit, guaranteeing what is to come.
Therefore we are always confident ...*
2 Corinthians 5:5, 6

We can never give up hope with our
children. God is not finished with them
or us yet, and our hope can sometimes
mean the difference between a relationship that fades away to nothing and a
restoration between parent and child.

HOPING EVEN WHEN ...

*" ... In this world you will have trouble. But
take heart! I have overcome the world."*
John 16:33

Yes, we can hope even when we don't see
any tangible results in our relationship
with our child. We don't know what
God might be doing for him or her. We
don't know how God is using what we
try to do for him or her, even when we
don't see the results.

ALL ACTS OF LOVE BEAR FRUIT

*Let us not become weary in doing
good, for at the proper time we will
reap a harvest if we do not give up.*
Galatians 6:9

Often we cannot see the fruits of our
work, and so think our work has been
in vain. In God's service somewhere
all our acts of love bear fruit, and some
heart receives their blessing and joy.

MY NAME ON THE INVITATION

"Come to me, all you who are weary and
burdened, and I will give you rest."
Matthew 11:28

*R*SVP

Christ said, "Come unto Me,
All ye that labour
And are heavy laden
And I will give you rest."
These were just beautiful words to
me – no more – until I realized
that my name was on the invitation.

HAPPINESS IS POSSIBLE

> *May the God of hope fill you with*
> *all joy and peace as you trust in him,*
> *so that you may overflow with hope*
> *by the power of the Holy Spirit.*
> Romans 15:13

*H*appiness and hope are so closely inter-twined that it seems as though if we just grab onto that little bit of hope, it pulls us up out of the pit enough to remember that happiness is possible.

THE COMFORTING ARMS OF GOD

*"So with you: Now is your time of grief, but
I will see you again and you will rejoice,
and no one will take away your joy."*
John 16:22

My prayer for you is that you will
feel the comforting arms of God
around you, giving you hope for the
future. God can take your trouble and
change it into a treasure. Your sorrow
can be exchanged for joy, not just a
momentary smile, but a deep, new joy.

A SPIRIT OF PARDON

*Humble yourselves, therefore, under
God's mighty hand, that he may lift
you up in due time. Cast all your
anxiety on him because he cares for you.*
1 Peter 5:6, 7

Offer yourself to God and ask for
a spirit of pardon so your being will
be restored. Tears and sorrow come,
but each time God will be there
to remind you that He cares.

THE GOLDEN CROWN OF GLORY

To him who overcomes, I will give the right to sit with me on my throne, just as I overcame and sat down with my Father on his throne.
Revelation 3:21

We know the iron crown of suffering precedes the golden crown of glory.

GIVE TO GOD

But this is what the LORD says: "Yes, captives will be taken from warriors, and plunder retrieved from the fierce; I will contend with those who contend with you, and your children I will save."
Isaiah 49:25

Give your son or daughter to God, and then focus on getting your life together. Keep in mind that you are not responsible for what you cannot control.

MAY 28

GENUINE HEALING

*... "You must serve faithfully and
wholeheartedly in the fear of the LORD."*
2 Chronicles 19:9

*R*emember, God only called you to be
faithful; He did not call you to be
successful! Genuine healing is a
process, and takes us a long, long time.

MAY 29

THINK ABOUT SUCH THINGS

*... we take captive every thought
to make it obedient to Christ.*
2 Corinthians 10:5

*F*inally, brothers, whatever is true,
whatever is noble, whatever is right,
whatever is pure, whatever is lovely,
whatever is admirable – if anything is
excellent or praiseworthy – think about
such things. Philippians 4:8 NIV

MAY 30

IF YOU HAVE HOPE

For everything that was written in the past was written to teach us, so that through endurance and the encouragement of the Scriptures we might have hope.
Romans 15:4

*T*o have hope is to be a winner. Even when you are last in the race, even when all of your friends' children are models of perfection and spiritual holiness while yours have bitterly disappointed you, you can be a winner if you have hope.

MAY 31

VICTORY THROUGH HOPE

"However, I consider my life worth nothing to me, if only I may finish the race and complete the task the Lord Jesus has given me ... "
Acts 20:24

Your child is in God's hands – let Him take the burden of your sorrow and build victory through your hope. This isn't the end of your life. It's the beginning of your future.

JUNE

JUNE 1

CONSTRUCTIVE IN PAIN

The LORD your God has blessed you in all the work of your hands. He has watched over your journey through this vast desert. These forty years the LORD your God has been with you, and you have not lacked anything.
Deuteronomy 2:7

In your calendar of recovery, June
is your month to be constructive
in your pain, to find an oasis
in the desert of your hurt.

JUNE 2

A LITTLE LOVE

*He turned the desert into pools of water
and the parched ground into flowing springs.*
Psalm 107:35

A little love, a little trust,
A soft impulse, a sudden dream,
And life as dry as desert dust
Is fresher than a mountain stream.

CHANNELS FOR SHARING

*"This is what the LORD Almighty
says: 'Administer true justice; show mercy
and compassion to one another.'"*
Zechariah 7:9

God has given us two hands – one to
receive with and the other with which to
give. We are cisterns made for hoarding –
we are channels made for sharing.

JUNE 4

ONE TOUCH OF ROSY SUNSET

*... offer your bodies as living
sacrifices, holy and pleasing to God –
this is your spiritual act of worship.*
Romans 12:1

If you can put one touch of rosy sunset
into the life of another, you should feel
that you have worked with God.

SPRINGS OF LIVING WATER

... *"Everyone who drinks this water will be thirsty again, but whoever drinks the water I give him will never thirst. Indeed, the water I give him will become in him a spring of water welling up to eternal life."*
John 4:13, 14

*G*od can give you springs of living water that will bubble up from within you like joy that is percolating from inside you and bubbling up to refresh others around you.

JUNE 6

SPARKLING JEWELS FROM GOD

The wild animals honor me, the jackals
and the owls, because I provide water in
the desert and streams in the wasteland,
to give drink to my people, my chosen.
Isaiah 43:20

Have you ever been in the
desert at night and seen the
glistening stars twinkle brightly?
All around us we can find sparkling
jewels from God scattered in our dark
places – if only we look for them.

JUNE 7

HOW MANY WAYS

And we urge you, brothers, warn those who are idle, encourage the timid, help the weak, be patient with everyone. Make sure that nobody pays back wrong for wrong, but always try to be kind to each other and to everyone else.
1 Thessalonians 5:14, 15

See how many ways you can find to put color and life and water and contentment in others' lives, and you will find your desert will bloom — and so will you.

JUNE 8

NO JOY WITHOUT SORROW

I want to know Christ and the power of his resurrection and the fellowship of sharing in his sufferings, becoming like him in his death, and so, somehow, to attain to the resurrection from the dead.
Philippians 3:10, 11

*T*here is no oil without
squeezing the olives,
No wine without
pressing the grapes,
No fragrance without
crushing the flowers,
And no real joy without sorrow.

JOY IN AN ORDINARY DAY

When I consider your heavens, the work of your fingers, the moon and the stars, which you have set in place ... O LORD, our Lord, how majestic is your name in all the earth!
Psalm 8:3, 9

Sometimes the less sophisticated you are, the easier it is to find joy in an ordinary day. Practice looking for joy, and you will be surprised at all the places you find it.

INEXPENSIVE JOY

*I will praise you, O LORD, with all my
heart; I will tell of all your wonders. I
will be glad and rejoice in you; I will
sing praise to your name, O Most High.*
Psalm 9:1, 2

Joy doesn't have to be expensive.
You don't have to sell your family jewels
(if you have any) to buy joy. Joy is
thoughtfulness. Joy is caring. Joy is
saying, "Thank you, God," for life.

JUNE 11

SHARE JOY

And over all these virtues put on love, which binds them all together in perfect unity.
Colossians 3:14

*L*et those around you who love you share joy with you. The oasis built in your desert by your family can be the best one of all.

A WORD OF ENCOURAGEMENT

*Do not be anxious about anything, but
in everything, by prayer and petition,
with thanksgiving, present your requests
to God. And the peace of God, which
transcends all understanding, will guard
your hearts and your minds in Christ Jesus.*
Philippians 4:6, 7

Anxious hearts are very heavy but a
word of encouragement does wonders!
Proverbs 12:25 TLB

JUNE 13

LITTLE GESTURES

... respect those who work hard among you, who are over you in the Lord and who admonish you. Hold them in the highest regard in love because of their work ...
1 Thessalonians 5:12, 13

Most discouraged people do not need professional help; they need those little appreciations, approvals, or admirations that can lift their spirits and give them courage to keep on coping with the nitty-gritty of life.

JUNE 14

RECOGNIZE THE JOY

Therefore encourage one another and build each other up, just as in fact you are doing.
1 Thessalonians 5:11

Joy from loved ones can be a very simple and very powerful encourager. Recognize the joy held out to you by those who love you, and think of how you can be a spirit lifter to someone else.

JUNE 15

HOPE DEFERRED

*Against all hope, Abraham in hope believed
and so became the father of many nations ...*
Romans 4:18

After you have given your problem
to God, you can then sit back and
expect Him to work on it. Giving
your burden to God is where faith
comes in, and hope is always in the
picture, even if it is hope deferred.

JUNE 16

YOUR JOY BOX

*... to bestow on them a crown of
beauty instead of ashes, the oil of
gladness instead of mourning ...*
Isaiah 61:3

Do you have a grouch box instead
of a joy box? Throw it away
and stuff your joy box full.

JUNE 17

ALL THE GOOD THINGS

... Be careful to do what is right in the eyes of everybody. If it is possible, as far as it depends on you, live at peace with everyone.
Romans 12:17, 18

*T*ake a friend to lunch. Talk about all the good things in the world. Or make up with an old friend.

A SELFLESS DEED

"But when you give to the needy, do not let your left hand know what your right hand is doing, so that your giving may be in secret. Then your Father, who sees what is done in secret, will reward you."
Matthew 6:3, 4

Do an anonymous good deed.

NO TRIAL RUNS

*Now that you have purified
yourselves by obeying the truth ... love
one another deeply, from the heart.*
1 Peter 1:22

*N*obody is a perfect parent, and there
are no trial runs at parenting. We just
love our kids and do our best – God
doesn't demand anything more.

JUNE 20

SPREADING LOVE

Your love has given me great joy and encouragement, because you, brother, have refreshed the hearts of the saints.
Philemon verse 7

Call two favorite people and tell them how much you love them.

JUNE 21

ACCEPT GOD'S FORGIVENESS

If we confess our sins, he is faithful
and just and will forgive us our sins
and purify us from all unrighteousness.
1 John 1:9

Stop blaming yourself for decisions your child has made. Accept God's forgiveness, and rejoice that straightening your kid out is His responsibility, not yours.

NOTES OF APPRECIATION

Pleasant words are a honeycomb,
sweet to the soul and healing to the bones.
Proverbs 16:24

Write notes of appreciation to people who have been a special help or influence in your life.

BEAUTY ALONG THE WAY

When I consider your heavens, the work of your fingers, the moon and the stars, which you have set in place, what is man that you are mindful of him, the son of man that you care for him?
Psalm 8:3, 4

*T*ake a walk through a park, or explore a new area. See how much beauty you can find along the way.

BACK INTO THE SUNSHINE

*A friend loves at all times,
and a brother is born for adversity.*
Proverbs 17:17

When you are in the midst of a
black cloud, you can't see your way
out by yourself. You need someone
to hold your hand and guide you
back out into the sunshine.

TREAT YOURSELF

*Then I realized that it is good and proper
for a man to eat and drink, and to find
satisfaction in his toilsome labor under
the sun during the few days of life God
has given him – for this is his lot.*
Ecclesiastes 5:18

Spoil yourself a little. Buy
something you've always wanted.

YOUR OWN CHOICE

*Be joyful always; pray continually; give
thanks in all circumstances, for this is
God's will for you in Christ Jesus.*
1 Thessalonians 5:16-18

Realize that having a good day is really
your own choice. Give everyone a smile.

JUNE 27

A LIST OF BLESSINGS

*Your father's blessings are greater than
the blessings of the ancient mountains ...*
Genesis 49:26

Make a list of your blessings.
Include everything good that's
ever happened to you.

JUNE 28

HANG ON TO YOUR JOY

*Jesus Christ is the same
yesterday and today and forever.*
Hebrews 13:8

*E*ven those of us who have deep and
abiding joy which comes from the Lord
can sometimes lose its evidence under all
the garbage of life. Find your joy, and
hang on to it. See God's care for you
even in the small things in your life.

USE YOUR TIME WELL

"The eye is the lamp of the body. If your eyes are good, your whole body will be full of light. But if your eyes are bad, your whole body will be full of darkness. If then the light within you is darkness, how great is that darkness!"
Matthew 6:22, 23

If you spend a lot of time watching television, decide today you will watch one good program.

JUNE 30

BLOSSOMS OF JOY

(B)ecause you know that the testing of your faith develops perseverance. Perseverance must finish its work so that you may be mature and complete, not lacking anything.
James 1:3, 4

God can help you rise to the challenge of picking blossoms of joy from the midst of the thorns.

JULY

JULY 1

A MUCH-NEEDED BOOST

So then, just as you received Christ Jesus as Lord, continue to live in him, rooted and built up in him, strengthened in the faith as you were taught, and overflowing with thankfulness.
Colossians 2:6, 7

Hope and miracles are almost synonymous. Sometimes our hope seems to invite God to do a miracle in our lives. Sometimes our hope gets a much-needed boost from a miracle sent just for that purpose.

DIFFICULT BUT POSSIBLE

*That man should not think he will
receive anything from the Lord; he is a
double-minded man, unstable in all he does.*
James 1:7, 8

The winner says it may be difficult
but it is possible. The loser says it may
be possible but it is too difficult.

(Author unknown)

A PART OF GOD'S PLAN

*And without faith it is impossible to please
God, because anyone who comes to him must
believe that he exists and that he rewards
those who earnestly seek him.*

Hebrews 11:6

When we have hope, we are showing
that we trust God to work out the
situation. Trust is the only way we're
going to make it through and be a part
of God's marvelous plan for our child.

JULY 4

COMPLETE A TASK

*The end of a matter is better
than its beginning ...*
Ecclesiastes 7:8

Get out an unfinished
project and finish it.

LIVE IN THE PRESENT

*This is the day the Lord has made;
let us rejoice and be glad in it.*
Psalm 118:24

We cannot change the past, but we can ruin a perfectly good present by blaming ourselves for past mistakes.

CAST YOUR HURT ON HIM

*No, in all these things we are more than
conquerors through him who loved us.*
Romans 8:37

Lord, give me strength today. Place
within me the ability to cast my hurt
onto You. You have already borne all of
the hurt. You bore it on calvary. You
have fought the sin battle, and You won
the victory. Because of Calvary, this
victory is mine ... Now ... Today.

LEARN FROM MISTAKES

*When you were dead in your sins
and in the uncircumcision of your sinful
nature, God made you alive with
Christ. He forgave us all our sins ...*
Colossians 2:13

We have failed in many areas of
our lives, but failing doesn't make
us failures! We have to learn from
our mistakes, and learn how to
prevent them in the future.

GOD GIVES US GRACE

*And God is able to make all grace
abound to you, so that in all things
at all times, having all that you need,
you will abound in every good work.*
2 Corinthians 9:8

Each day God gives us the
grace for that day alone. You can
make it, one day at a time.

JULY 9

ENTRUST YOUR CHILD TO HIM

*Such confidence as this is ours through
Christ before God. Not that we are competent in
ourselves to claim anything for ourselves,
but our competence comes from God.*
2 Corinthians 3:4, 5

Lord, as I trust You this moment for my
own peace and assurance, I also trust
You to care for my child's needs.

MOVE OUT OF PAST FAILURES

> *... Jesus Christ, who gave himself for*
> *us to redeem us from all wickedness and*
> *to purify for himself a people that are his*
> *very own, eager to do what is good.*
> Titus 2:13, 14

You cannot go back and unscramble eggs. There is no way to undo what has been done. Let's move out of our past failures, and starting with our scrambled eggs, learn how to make soufflés!

HE IS IN CONTROL

... God has said, "Never will I leave
you; never will I forsake you." So we
say with confidence, "The Lord is my
helper; I will not be afraid ... "
Hebrews 13:5, 6

My prayer for you is that God will
wrap you in His special comfort blanket
and make you know He is in control
of the situation. You are not alone
out there. Just nestle in His arms.

JULY 12

PARDON AND LOVE

*And God raised us up with Christ and seated
us with him in the heavenly realms in Christ
Jesus, in order that in the coming ages he might
show the incomparable riches of his grace,
expressed in his kindness to us in Christ Jesus.*
Ephesians 2:6, 7

*L*ord, have mercy and show Your
pardon and love to my child this day.

SHARE SOME SPECIAL THOUGHT

*He seldom reflects on the days of his life, because
God keeps him occupied with gladness of heart.*
Ecclesiastes 5:20

Stop what you are doing long enough
to enjoy the sunset, listen to a special
song that lifts you up, or pick up the
phone and share some special thought
with a caring friend.

JULY 14

DON'T STAY PARKED

*(H)aving canceled the written code,
with its regulations, that was against us
and that stood opposed to us; he took it
away, nailing it to the cross.*
Colossians 2:14

*G*od has promised to forgive and
cleanse us if we just ask. Don't
stay parked by your past sins.

RELAX MY MIND AND EMOTIONS

*You are forgiving and good, O Lord,
abounding in love to all who call to you.*
Psalm 86:5

Lord, forgive me my sins and
overlook my mistakes. Bring to me
your comfort. Relax all of the parts
of my mind and emotions that are
tense and burdened down.

A GUILT-FREE LIFE

*I have been crucified with Christ
and I no longer live, but Christ lives
in me. The life I live in the body, I
live by faith in the Son of God ...*
Galatians 2:20

*G*ood news! Jesus was nailed to a cross
so that you could stop nailing yourself
to a cross. Accept His forgiveness and
live a guilt-free life from here on out!

REACH OUT AND ACCEPT

*But because of his great love for us, God
who is rich in mercy, made us alive with
Christ even when we were dead in transgressions — it is by grace you have been saved.*
Ephesians 2:4, 5

We must be frank and honest with God
on what we have done wrong. Then we
must relinquish it to God, give to Him
our failures, and reach out and accept
God's cleansing forgiveness.

CLEAN HANDS AND A PURE HEART

Come near to God and he will come near to you.
Wash your hands ... and purify your hearts ...
and he will lift you up.
James 4:8, 10

*L*ord, I need Your help. Let me come to
You with clean hands and a pure heart.
Help me live where I can be free to serve
You and experience joy in my life.

ACCEPTANCE BASED ON GRACE

*For it is by grace you have been saved,
through faith — and this not from
yourselves, it is the gift of God.*
Ephesians 2:8

Even when our child's actions stab
our hearts with pain, we need to
remember that God loves him or
her and His acceptance is based
on grace, not perfection.

JULY 20

FOREVER WORTHY

*There is no fear in love. But perfect love drives
out fear, because fear has to do with punish-
ment. The one who fears is not made perfect in
love. We love because he first loved us.*
1 John 4:18, 19

Dear God, I have sinned against
heaven and against You. I am no
longer worthy to be called Your child.

My child, I know, I know.
... But My Son is forever worthy
to be called your Savior.

THE GOOD, SOLID FOOD

For the word of God is living and active.
Sharper than any double-edged sword,
it penetrates even to dividing soul and
spirit, joints and marrow ...
Hebrews 4:12

We need to keep the garbage out of our lives by feeding ourselves on the good, solid food of the Word of God.

JULY 22

WORTH LOVING

" ... *For I have not come to call
the righteous, but sinners.*"
Matthew 9:13

God believes you are worth loving, even
with your sins and with all your faults.

JULY 23

THE STING WILL HAVE GONE

*But rejoice that you participate in the
sufferings of Christ, so that you may be
overjoyed when his glory is revealed.*
1 Peter 4:13

*T*ry to see in your life the process of
healing that is taking place. Someday
you will look back and the sting will
have gone. You will actually be able to
enjoy your bittersweet memories.

GOD LOVES YOU SO MUCH

"For God so loved the world that he gave his one and only Son, that whoever believes in him shall not perish but have eternal life."
John 3:16

If you were the only sinner in the whole world, God loves you so much that Jesus would have died for you alone!

PRAY FOR GOD'S BEST

*To man belong the plans of the heart, but from
the LORD comes the reply of the tongue.*
Proverbs 16:1

So hang on, hold together, look up,
look inside, hang tight, and then after
you have done all that, sit back and let
God do the job. We are powerless to
do anything except love our kids and
pray for God's best for them.

MERCY

*[He] who has saved us and called us to
a holy life — not because of anything we
have done but because of his own purpose
and grace. This grace was given us in Christ
Jesus before the beginning of time ...*
2 Timothy 1:8, 9

Mercy is God *not* doing to us
what we so richly deserve.

THERE ARE OTHERS

*Brothers, as an example of patience in
the face of suffering, take the prophets
who spoke in the name of the Lord.*
James 5:10, 11

When we are hurting, we need to realize
that there are others who have been
through the agony we are experiencing,
and they can give us comfort and hope.

DEPRESSION HAPPENS TO US ALL

"Help us, O LORD ... for we rely on you ..."
2 Chronicles 14:11

Depression is a sometimes thing
That happens to us all!
But none can help like Jesus,
When depression comes to call.

(Author unknown)

JULY 29

THE HARD CRUSHES OF LIFE

*Carry each other's burdens, and in this
way you will fulfill the law of Christ.*
Galatians 6:2

Christians can be like a sack of
grapes, able to comfort each other,
pressing together to provide a soft,
loving, warm place to cushion each
other in the hard crushes of life.

JULY 30

VISIT A FRIEND

*But it is you ... my companion, my close friend,
with whom I once enjoyed sweet fellowship ...*
Psalm 55:13

One way to beat the blues – visit a
friend you haven't seen in a long while.

JULY 31

LIFE WILL GO ON

*He himself bore our sins in his body
on the tree, so that we might die to
sins and live for righteousness; by
his wounds you have been healed.*
1 Peter 2:24

*I*n time your hurt will heal, your
heart will start the mending process,
life will go on, and so will you!

AUGUST

AUGUST 1

YOUR ATTITUDE MAKES THE DIFFERENCE!

And he who searches our hearts knows the mind of the Spirit, because the Spirit intercedes for the saints in accordance with God's will.
Romans 8:27

August is dedicated to everyone who is battling for weight or age control. Remember, no matter how old or how heavy you are, no matter how successful or not your diet is, your attitude makes the difference!

SOMEDAY

"But while they were on their way to buy the oil, the bridegroom arrived. The virgins who were ready went in with him to the wedding banquet. And the door was shut. Therefore keep watch, because you do not know the day or the hour."
Matthew 25:10, 13

Live every day as if it were your last ... and someday you'll be right.

AUGUST 3

TAP INTO A BOUNDLESS FOUNTAIN

*A happy heart makes the face cheerful,
but heartache crushes the spirit.*
Proverbs 15:13

*I*nject some humor into your life!
There are so many ways to do it. By
letting ourselves become children again,
we can tap into a boundless fountain
within us, learning to laugh all over
again. Kids laugh out of sheer joy;
they don't need a good "reason".

AUGUST 4

A TAPE AROUND THE HEART

This is how we know who the children of God are and who the children of the devil are: Anyone who does not do what is right is not a child of God; nor is anyone who does not love his brother.
1 John 3:10

When God measures a person, He puts a tape around the heart, not the head.

BE IMPULSIVE

Take me away with you — let us hurry!
... We rejoice and delight in you ...
Song of Songs 1:4

Quit taking yourself so seriously. Do
some fun things, just because you want
to be impulsive and adventurous.

AGING: AN ADVENTURE

*When Abram was ninety-nine years old, the
LORD appeared to him and said, "I am God
Almighty; walk before me and be blameless. I
will confirm my covenant between me and you
and will greatly increase your numbers."*
Genesis 17:1, 2

Think of aging as a marvelous
adventure in uncharted lands, lands
you will only pass through once –
so enjoy them to the fullest.

AUGUST 7

SHARED JOYS

*I rejoice greatly in the Lord that at last
you have renewed your concern for me ...*
Philippians 4:10

Reflect on shared joys and
rewarding friendships.

THAT CHILDLIKE ESSENCE

... *"I tell you the truth, unless you change
and become like little children, you will
never enter the kingdom of heaven."*
Matthew 18:3

*B*e a child again! Let yourself
recapture that childlike essence.
We can be at peace with ourselves
and forever young at heart as we
grow through this stage together.

BELONGING TO

*If we claim to have fellowship with him
yet walk in the darkness, we lie and do
not live by the truth. But if we walk in
the light, as he is in the light, we have
fellowship with one another, and the blood of
Jesus, his Son, purifies us from all sin.*
1 John 1:6, 7

Don't worry about *who* you
are, but *whose* you are.

AUGUST 10

CHILDLIKE NOT CHILDISH

*Like the crackling of thorns under the
pot, so is the laughter of fools ...*
Ecclesiastes 7:6

It is time to think of ways to
inject fun into your life. It's
wonderful to be childlike. Just
don't confuse it with being childish!

GROWING OLDER

*Keep yourselves in God's love as you
wait for the mercy of our Lord Jesus
Christ to bring you to eternal life.*
Jude verse 21

How to tell you are growing older:
– You feel like the night before,
and you haven't been anywhere.
– You know all the answers, but
nobody asks you the questions.
– You turn out the lights for economic
reasons instead of romantic ones.
– You stop looking forward
to your next birthday.

LESS THAN YOUR BEST

*So whether you eat or drink or whatever
you do, do it all for the glory of God.*
1 Corinthians 10:31

It's no disgrace to fail, but it's
a sin to do less than your best.

THE RICHES OF OUR LOVED ONES

Let the peace of Christ rule in your hearts, since as members of one body you were called to peace. And be thankful.
Colossians 3:15

We should appreciate the life God has given us, and we should cultivate the riches of our loved ones around us.

GET PERSPECTIVE

*Cast all your anxiety on him
because he cares for you.*
1 Peter 5:7

We need to step back from our own
problems, get some perspective,
and turn our liabilities into assets.

PARENTAL CONSOLATION

*Rather, as servants of God we commend our-
selves in every way: in great endurance;
in troubles, hardships and distresses ...*
2 Corinthians 6:4

*T*houghts to console parents whose kids
have already moved back in:
– Now that the kids are back, you don't
have to eat leftovers. There aren't any.
– Remember when you worried because
you didn't know where your children
were? Now, you know. They're
back in their own rooms.
– Before they left, the kids were deduct-
ible. Now, they're just taxing.

AUGUST 16

LOOK CREATIVELY

*And we know that in all things God works
for the good of those who love him, who have
been called according to his purpose.*
Romans 8:28

Let's not wallow in our difficulties
anymore; that doesn't help at all.
Instead, let's look at our situation
creatively and see the humor and
benefits of going through disaster.

WISHING WITHOUT WORK

What good is it, my brothers, if a man claims to have faith but has no deeds? Can such faith save him?
James 2:14

Wishing without work is like fishing without bait.

AUGUST 18

A UNIQUE OPPORTUNITY

*Moses was eighty years old and Aaron
eighty-three when they spoke to Pharaoh.*
Exodus 7:7

Perspective is how we look at life,
ourselves, and our problems. Some look
at aging as a unique opportunity for fun.

GIVEN UP RUNNING

My times are in your hands ...
Psalm 31:15

I've given up running for the bus,
as it leaves faster than it used to.

GOD CARES

*" ... And surely I am with you
always, to the very end of the age."*
Matthew 28:20

Keep in mind that you are not
alone; there are thousands of others
in just the same kind of circumstances
you find yourself. God will take care
of you, just as He cares for others.

SAFE BUT SORRY?

*My soul finds rest in God alone; my
salvation comes from him. He alone is
my rock and my salvation; he is my
fortress, I will never be shaken.*
Psalm 62:1, 2

A ship in harbor is safe, but that
is not what ships are built for.

RIGHT BESIDE US

*His divine power has given us everything
we need for life and godliness through
our knowledge of him who called us by
his own glory and goodness.*
2 Peter 1:3

Remember, the Lord is right beside us,
encouraging, admonishing, and setting
goals for us. Give your best to God, and
then forget about your pounds and
years. No one is too heavy or too
old to need and receive God's love.

AUGUST 23

HUMOR IN AGING

Do not say, "Why were the old days better than these?" For it is not wise to ask such questions.
Ecclesiastes 7:10

I ran into a classmate the other day, and she had aged so much she didn't even recognize me.

DANCING INSTEAD OF MARCHING

> *The Sovereign LORD is my strength;*
> *he makes my feet like the feet of a deer,*
> *he enables me to go on the heights.*
> Habakkuk 3:19

If you can look at the inexorable march of time with humor, you can dance through life instead of marching.

WELL-USED

*If you point these things out to the brothers, you
will be a good minister of Christ Jesus, brought
up in the truths of the faith and of the good
teaching that you have followed.*
1 Timothy 4:6

A Bible that is falling apart probably
belongs to someone whose life is not.

LEAVE THE REST TO THE LORD

For everything that was written in the past was written to teach us, so that through endurance and the encouragement of the Scriptures we might have hope.
Romans 15:4

Being overweight is no excuse to check out of life and give up. Work at your weight the best you can, leave the rest up to the Lord, and learn to treat your weight problem with humor. It will help, and even though it doesn't burn very many calories to laugh, it does make dieting more enjoyable.

AUGUST 27

ONE DAY AT A TIME

He [God] has made everything beautiful
in its time. He has also set eternity in the hearts
of men; yet they cannot fathom
what God has done from beginning to end.
Ecclesiastes 3:11

Perhaps the best thing about the future
is that it comes just one day at a time.

JOYOUS DETERMINATION

A cheerful look brings joy to the heart, and good news gives health to the bones.
Proverbs 15:30

Don't give up on yourself if you are struggling with a diet. Remember not to have grim determination but joyous determination. Being able to laugh at your dieting struggles will take some of the pain away.

THE BOTTOM LINE

A man's steps are directed by the LORD. How then can anyone understand his own way?
Proverbs 20:24

What is the bottom line on aging and dieting? The bottom line is that your future is in God's hands, not yours.

HIS FREE GIFT

*(F)or all have sinned and fall short
of the glory of God, and are justified
freely by his grace through the
redemption that came by Christ Jesus.*
Romans 3:23, 24

Jesus Christ won't be concerned
about our age or our weight, but
about whether we accepted His free
gift of eternal life, which He purchased
with His own blood on the cross.

AUGUST 31

YOU WILL WIN

He died for us so that, whether we are awake or asleep, we may live together with him.
1 Thessalonians 5:10

You are growing, you are changing, you are maturing; you will win, with God's help.

SEPTEMBER

SEPTEMBER 1

BUILDING AND REMEMBERING

*The fruit of the righteous is a tree of
life, and he who wins souls is wise.*
Proverbs 11:30

In our calendar of recovery, September is
our month for building and remembering the experiences our children will
carry with them throughout their lives.
It is a necessary part of growing up,
and a necessary part of a parent's reflec-
tions on all of the precious yesterdays
he or she shared with a child who is,
perhaps, estranged and far away today.

A HEALING LAUGHTER

"Others, like seed sown on good soil, hear the word, accept it, and produce a crop – thirty, sixty or even a hundred times what was sown."
Mark 4:20

Give love a chance and make September your month to hear a healing, soothing laughter that paves the way for restoration. It's worth it!

SEPTEMBER 3

WIND IT UP

*I press on toward the goal to win the
prize for which God has called me
heavenward in Christ Jesus.*
Philippians 3:13

You can't turn back the clock,
but you can wind it up again.

BUILDING LAUGHTER

Let me hear joy and gladness ...
Psalm 51:8

Are you building laughter in your home? Is it alive with music and singing and a clock that chimes, and some life? Living in a house can be so dull if you are not alive yourself.

SEPTEMBER 5

WHAT NOT TO DO

*And do not grieve the Holy Spirit
of God, with whom you were
sealed for the day of redemption.*
Ephesians 4:30

Knowing what to do is important,
but never more important than
knowing what *not* to do.

THE WAYS TO SHOW LOVE

Be devoted to one another in brotherly love.
Honor one another above yourselves.
Romans 12:10

Many are the ways to show love. A positive reinforcement stated, a note written, a diaper changed, a meal cooked, a soft word spoken, a tub of dirty clothes washed, a pat of reassurance given, a kiss of unrestrained passion shared, a car repaired, a flower sent, a loving spirit lived!

HE IS MINE

"I give them eternal life, and they shall never perish; no one can snatch them out of my hand."
John 10:28

One day a father was talking to a friend about his son, who had caused great heartache. The friend said, "If he were my son, I would kick him out." The father thought for a moment, then said, "Yes, if he were your son, so would I. But he is not your son; he is mine and I can't do it."

WAITING TO HEAR

*Perfume and incense bring joy to the
heart, and the pleasantness of one's
friend springs from his earnest counsel.*
Proverbs 27:9

*F*riends are those rare people
who ask you how you are and
then wait to hear the answer.

SEPTEMBER 9

LOVE PROTECTS, TRUSTS AND HOPES

And over all these virtues put on love, which
binds them all together in perfect unity.
Colossians 3:14

*L*ove always:
Protects — I want to take the
hurt for my child. Instead,
I will protect and love him.
Trusts — I trust, even when my husband
travels a lot and faces life's temptations.
Hopes — We still share our
dreams for life together.

LAUGHTER IN THE WALLS

*He will yet fill your mouth with laughter
and your lips with shouts of joy.*
Job 7:9

Get some laughter into your life
today, and then when the house is
empty, you will remember all the
laughter from yesterdays full of
laughter. It's in the walls.

SEPTEMBER 11

IN THEIR POSITION

*Live in harmony with one another. Do not be
proud, but be willing to associate with people
of low position. Do not be conceited.*
Romans 12:16

*T*he easiest thing to decide is
what you would do if you were
in somebody else's shoes.

SEPTEMBER 12

A CHILD'S HEART

Train a child in the way he should go, and when he is old he will not turn from it.
Proverbs 22:6

Whatever you write on the heart of a child, no water can wash it away.

(Author unknown)

TOO PRECIOUS TO WASTE

*He settles the barren woman in her home as a
happy mother of children. Praise the LORD.*
Psalm 113:9

Be grateful for what you and your child
had and treasure it. It is too precious to
waste. And use what you had before to
help you bear what you have today.

SEPTEMBER 14

ON THE PALMS OF MY HANDS

"See, I have engraved you on
the palms of my hands ... "
Isaiah 49:16

God's palm can be a place of rest for you because God's loving care extends to all of us. When we cast our care upon Him, He cares for us. In the bible God reminds us, *"See, I have [carved] you on the palms of my hands."* Isaiah 49:16 NIV

SEPTEMBER 15

FAME IS NOT SUCCESS

Humble yourselves, therefore,
under God's mighty hand, that
he may lift you up in due time.
1 Peter 5:6

Don't confuse fame with success. Madonna is one. Helen Keller is the other.

BUILDING MEMORIES

*Let us hold unswervingly to the hope we
profess, for he who promised is faithful.*
Hebrews 10:23

*I*n the process of building memories,
we suffer some, too. It is up to God to
pick us up, brush us off, kiss away our
tears, and reassure us of His love, no
matter what we have endured.

SEPTEMBER 17

UNCONDITIONAL LOVE

> ... (L)ive a life of love, just as Christ
> loved us and gave himself up for us as a
> fragrant offering and sacrifice to God.
> Ephesians 5:2

I know it hurts to love the child who
has turned on you, whose actions pierce
your heart sharper than any sword. But
God's love is unconditional. Is yours?

SEPTEMBER 18

THE UNIQUE BOND

*... your sons will be like olive shoots
around your table. Thus is the man
blessed who fears the LORD.*
Psalm 128:3, 4

*T*hink back to the good times
you and your child had. Think
back to the spiritual and emotional
bond you two shared that is the
unique bond of parent and child.

SEPTEMBER 19

HIDING PANIC

*May the Lord direct your hearts into
God's love and Christ's perseverance.*
2 Thessalonians 3:5

*L*eadership is the ability to
hide your panic from others.

NO STRINGS ATTACHED

*Be kind and compassionate to one
another, forgiving each other, just
as in Christ God forgave you.*
Ephesians 4:32

*F*ace your child, forgive him or her,
love him, and welcome him with open
arms. You might even get hurt again,
but you don't have to agree with your
child, just to love her and reassure her
of your love, which is as unconditional
as that of God – no strings attached.

LIFE WITHOUT RISK

> ... *"Wake up, O sleeper, rise from the dead, and Christ will shine on you."*
> Ephesians 5:14

Life without risk is not worth living.

SEPTEMBER 22

THE REWARD

And now these three remain: faith, hope and love. But the greatest of these is love.
1 Corinthians 13:13

*T*here is a risk to loving your child: You are vulnerable. You can get hurt. But the reward and the responsibility can give you a maturity, a close love, and a relationship nothing can ever replace.

JUST TRUST HIM

> *Let your hand rest on the man at*
> *your right hand, the son of man*
> *you have raised up for yourself.*
> Psalm 80:17

God knows how much you are hurting because of what your child has said or done. And God knows that you are not perfect, too. Leave the results up to God, and just trust Him with your child.

SEPTEMBER 24

NOT IN ONE DAY

*Those who sow in tears will reap with
songs of joy. He who goes out weeping,
carrying seed to sow, will return with
songs of joy, carrying sheaves with him.*
Psalm 126:5, 6

Some, like farmers, need to learn that
they can't sow and reap the same day.

SEPTEMBER 25

I HAVE MY GOD

God blessed them and said to them,
"Be fruitful and increase in number;
fill the earth and subdue it ... "
Genesis 1:28

Would I have been better off if I had never married, had never had children? ... No! In spite of all the tragedy, and all the heartache, and all the sorrow, I wouldn't trade my life for any other life in the world. I have the laughter to remind me of the good times, and I have my God, who gives me the strength to survive the tragedy, and the joy to appreciate my blessings!

THE LAUGHTER WILL BUILD YOU STRONG

... *"My grace is sufficient for you, for my power is made perfect in weakness."*
2 Corinthians 12:9

*T*ake the risk, let yourself go, love your child. No matter what suffering you go through later, the laughter you experience now will build you strong for those times of testing.

SEPTEMBER 27

AN IMPORTANT STEP

> *... if anyone competes as an athlete,*
> *he does not receive the victor's crown*
> *unless he competes according to the rules.*
> 2 Timothy 2:5

*L*earning to forgive, to love with
no strings attached, and to be willing
to risk being hurt again, is an
important step in your recovery.

SEPTEMBER 28

OPEN YOUR HEART

*"Ask and it will be given to you; seek and
you will find; knock and the door will be
opened to you. For everyone who asks
receives; he who seeks finds; and to him
who knocks, the door will be opened."*
Matthew 7:7, 8

Open your heart right now,
and expect that God is going
to restore your child to you.

SEPTEMBER 29

STRENGTH DEVELOPED

And she [Hannah] made a vow, saying, "O LORD Almighty, if you will only look upon your servant's misery and ... not forget your servant but give her a son, then I will give him to the LORD for all the days of his life ... "
1 Samuel 1:11

It's so much easier to fight for your child when he has gone astray if you can call on that strength developed through laughter.

SEPTEMBER 30

NEW LOVE

*... live a life of love, just as Christ loved
us and gave himself up for us as a fragrant
offering and sacrifice to God.*
Ephesians 5:2

God will restore your love for each other,
and He will be faithful to nurture your
new love, a love which has weathered
the storms of adversity and survived.

OCTOBER

OCTOBER 1

ACCEPT GOD'S WILL

*... "Our Father in heaven, hallowed be
your name, your kingdom come, your will
be done on earth as it is in heaven."*
Matthew 6:9, 10

*I*n October, learn to accept God's will.
Learn to say, in the face of unbelievable
chaos and tragedy, "Whatever, Lord!"

OCTOBER 2

GOD'S GRACE AND LOVE ARE SUFFICIENT

But he said to me, "My grace is sufficient for you, for my power is made perfect in weakness."
2 Corinthians 12:9

The encouragement I can give you for October is remember that God's grace and love are sufficient for any situation you could ever experience. God will listen to your fears and assure you that he is in control.

BASED IN THE LOVE OF GOD

*It [Love] is not rude, it is not
self-seeking, it is not easily angered, it keeps
no record of wrongs. Love never fails ...*
1 Corinthians 13:5, 8

My family and I know we love
each other. We know that our love,
based in the love of God, has with-
stood the test and is stronger than
ever. No matter what happens, we
love each other, no strings attached.

MISERY DOES NOT HAVE TO BE PERMANENT

You need to persevere so that when you have done the will of God, you will receive what he has promised.
Hebrews 10:36

I now know through my own experience that misery does not have to be permanent. There is recovery. Life is worth living again, and I am stronger through what I went through.

OCTOBER 5

A RICH LIFE

*Let us not become weary in doing
good, for at the proper time we will
reap a harvest if we do not give up.*
Galatians 6:9

It is true that a life in Christ is a life rich
in love and Christian companionship.

OCTOBER 6

IN GOD'S HANDS

..."*The gracious hand of our God is
on everyone who looks to him ...*"
Ezra 8:22

I wouldn't have chosen this life,
but I wouldn't trade it for anything.
My life is in God's hands, and I
can't get much safer than that!

A REMEDY

These men are grumblers and fault-finders ... But you, dear friends, build yourselves up in your most holy faith and pray in the Holy Spirit.
Jude verse 16, 20

Don't find fault. Find a remedy.

OCTOBER 8

"WHATEVER, LORD!"

He [Job] replied, " ... Shall we accept good from God, and not trouble?"
Job 2:10

We all have trials in our lives when we flail out at God and ask, "Why did you let this terrible thing happen to me?" And it is then that we should turn it around and say, "Whatever, Lord!"

WITH YOU DURING THE TRIAL

*Do not be anxious about anything, but in
everything, by prayer and petition, with
thanksgiving, present your requests to God.
And the peace of God, which transcends all
understanding, will guard your hearts
and your minds in Christ Jesus.*
Philippians 4:6, 7

Nothing comes into the life of a
Christian that God doesn't know about.
Then you can just relax and kick it out
of gear for a while and know that God
will be with you during the trial.

OCTOBER 10

INTO THE HEALING STAGE

*This is the confidence we have in
approaching God: that if we ask anything
according to his will, he hears us.*
1 John 5:14

*W*hen "Whatever, Lord!" replaces
"Why me?" then you can know that
you are on the way to growing through
your trial or your crunch time. You are
finally into the healing stage. You have
survived the panic situation, and you
are moving into normalcy again.

OCTOBER 11

A NORMAL STATE

*For the LORD watches over the
way of the righteous, but the way
of the wicked will perish.*
Psalm 1:6

Sometimes we wonder if there really is a
normal state after the trauma we have
come through. Robert Frost said he
could sum up everything he had learned
about life in three words: "It goes on!"

SOME PERSPECTIVE

*So then, just as you received Christ Jesus
as Lord, continue to live in him ...*
Colossians 2:6

A friend wrote me that we should
live as if Christ died yesterday, arose
this morning, and is coming back
today! That helps us get some
perspective on all the areas around
us which seem like disaster zones.

LIFE GOES ON

*... Though I have fallen, I will rise. Though I
sit in darkness, the LORD will be my light.*
Micah 7:8

The human spirit can survive
pain, loss, death, taxes, and life
goes on, and on, and on.

OCTOBER 14

IT WORKED TOGETHER FOR GOOD

(B)ecause you know that the testing of your faith develops perseverance. Perseverance must finish its work so that you may be mature and complete, not lacking anything.
James 1:3, 4

Your experience in the furnace will not last forever. In time, you will be able to look back and see how it all worked together for good in your life.

OCTOBER 15

KEEP ON BELIEVING

Set your minds on things above,
not on earthly things.
Colossians 3:2

If I can but keep on believing
What I know in my heart to be true,
That darkness will
fade with the morning
And that this will pass away, too –
Then nothing in life can defeat me.

(Author unknown)

OCTOBER 16

JUST AS YOU ARE

*So God created man in his own image,
in the image of God he created him;
male and female he created them.*
Genesis 1:27

God's Love Letter to You
You are lovely in My eyes, and I created
you to be just as you are. Do not
criticize yourself or get down for
not being perfect in your own eyes.

A "SMILING HEART"

*Give thanks to the LORD, for he
is good; his love endures forever.*
Psalm 107:1

Do you ever have days when everything
is so marvelous that you want just any
small excuse to feel happy all over, like
your heart is smiling? When I was in the
depths of my suffering, I couldn't
imagine ever feeling like that again, but
it really is true that now I have days of a
"smiling heart". It was worth the suffering to make it through to that again!

ABDICATE GRACEFULLY

*Accept him ... without passing
judgment on disputable matters.*
Romans 14:1

As parents we have been on the top
of the totem pole, the decision makers
for so long, that it is difficult to learn
how to abdicate gracefully, to allow
our children to become adults.

OCTOBER 19

ACTIVE LISTENING

*"Give ear and come to me; hear me, that your
soul may live ..." declares the LORD.*
Isaiah 55:3, 8

Resolve not to argue over things that
have nothing to do with the situation at
hand. Then try some active listening.

LEARN TO LET GO

*... "For this reason a man will
leave his father and mother ..."*
Matthew 19:5

We have to learn to train up a child
and then let him go, but there is no
magic button that turns a parent who
has been the "omnipotent one" into
just one opinion in her child's life.

OCTOBER 21

WISDOM IN HIS WORD

*The fruit of the righteous is a tree of
life, and he who wins souls is wise.*
Proverbs 11:30

Ask the Lord for wisdom. Wisdom
is more important than knowledge.
It is that innate "sense" which comes
as a result of regular communion
with God, as well as from the wisdom
in His Word and our continued
walk in the light He gives to us.

A LOSING PROPOSITION

The simple inherit folly, but the prudent are crowned with knowledge.
Proverbs 14:18

We pay quite a high bill for being someone who has to be right all the time. And why? Being right can be a losing proposition. If you are right all of the time, you will intimidate people and make it so hard for them to remember the facts, or even attempt to share them with you.

THE PRESENCE OF THE LORD

You have made known to me the path of life;
you will fill me with joy in your presence ...
Psalm 16:11

*F*ocus on the Lord's presence.
Practice the presence of the Lord
in your life. It's surprising sometimes
how trivial our discussion may sound
to the Maker of the Universe. This
can be one giant step in the right direction toward restoration and recovery.

JUST BE QUIET

*He who guards his mouth and his
tongue keeps himself from calamity.*
Proverbs 21:23

Part of learning "Whatever, Lord!" is
learning that you don't have to be God
to your kids all the time. In fact, most
of the time, when relations are bad
anyhow, you should just be quiet.

OCTOBER 25

LOOK TO ME

*Do not conform any longer to the pattern
of this world, but be transformed by the
renewing of your mind. Then you will be
able to test and approve what God's will
is — his good, pleasing and perfect will.*
Romans 12:2

God's Love Letter to You
Dwell in My power and in My
love and be free! Be yourself! Don't
allow other people to run you. I
will guide you, if you let Me.
Look to Me for your answers.

SURVIVE WITH HUMOR

All the days of the oppressed are wretched, but the cheerful heart has a continual feast.
Proverbs 15:15

My encouraging word to all of you is that you develop a sense of humor to carry you through these days. Without a sense of humor you are doomed to despair, and yet with humor you can survive and actually enjoy the trip!

DAILY CLEANSING

*Therefore confess your sins to each other and
pray for each other so that you may be healed ...*
James 5:16

We all need daily cleansing. There
is no pocket of sin which is too
deep for God's love to restore us.

GIVE ALL TO GOD

Why should any living man complain when punished for his sins? Let us examine our ways ... and let us return to the LORD.
Lamentations 3:39, 40

Don't always look to complain to God about your life. Healing comes when we give God all the pieces.

GOD CAN BRING CONVICTION

"I will give them an undivided heart and put a new spirit in them; I will remove from them their heart of stone and give them a heart of flesh."
Ezekiel 11:19

God can take a heart of stone and make it a heart of flesh, and God can bring conviction to those who walk away from Christian training.

OCTOBER 30

GOD'S RESPONSIBILITY

" ... Love one another. As I have loved
you, so you must love one another."
John 13:34

God's Love Letter to You
Do not be concerned with yourself – you
are My responsibility. I will change you,
and you will hardly know it is happen-
ing. You are to love yourself and love
others simply because I love you.

OCTOBER 31

NO NIGHT WITHOUT DAWNING

*This is the message we have heard
from him and declare to you: God is
light; in him there is no darkness at all.*
1 John 1:5

I know God will break all the chains
That are binding me
tight in the darkness
And trying to fill me with fear –
For there is no night without dawning
And I know that my morning is near.

(Author unknown)

NOVEMBER

LET GO, AND CARE

Whoever loves his brother lives in the light, and there is nothing in him to make him stumble.
1 John 2:10

November's step to recovery is twofold: Let go, and care. With a combination like that, you will only succeed. Recovery is on the way. Wholeness is around the corner. Life is once again worth living.

NOVEMBER 2

LEARN TO LET GO

*Though an army besiege me, my heart
will not fear; though war break out
against me, even then will I be confident.*
Psalm 27:3

We can learn to let go – to be
thankful for what God has done,
to do our best, and then to let go:
of the pain, the suffering, the worry,
our children. When we have done
our best, we have to let our children
go and leave them in God's hands.

NOVEMBER 3

THE RETIREMENT PLAN

*Through him and for his name's
sake, we received grace and apostleship
to call people from among all the Gentiles
to the obedience that comes from faith.*
Romans 1:5

*W*orking for the Lord – it's great!
The pay isn't much, but the retire-
ment plan is just out of this world!

NOVEMBER 4

BEING THANKFUL

Let the peace of Christ rule in your hearts,
since as members of one body you were
called to peace. And be thankful.
Colossians 3:15

November is a month for snuggling
in against the cold weather, looking
back over the past month, and being
thankful for what God has given us
(sometimes we're thankful for what
God hasn't given us).

NOVEMBER 5

NOT TO

I am saying this for your own good, not to restrict you, but that you may live in a right way in undivided devotion to the Lord.
1 Corinthians 7:35

Letting Go

To let go is not to cut myself off; it's the realization that I can't control another. To let go is not to enable, but to allow learning from natural consequences. To let go is to admit powerlessness, which means the outcome is not in my hands. To let go is not to try to change or blame another; I can only change myself.

LEARN FROM THE PAST

*You have been set free from sin and
have become slaves to righteousness.*
Romans 6:18

*I*t's perfectly all right to look to the past
constructively, to learn from it, and to
appreciate where we've been. But it isn't
healthy to look back in regret and guilt.

NOVEMBER 7

IN HIS POWER

It is for freedom that Christ has set us free.
Stand firm, then, and do not let yourselves
be burdened again by a yoke of slavery.
Galatians 5:1

We have to be willing to "let go
of the string" and let God take our
balloons up in the sky, where they
are in His power, not our own.

NOVEMBER 8

CUTTING WISDOM TEETH

*Brothers, as an example of patience in the face
of suffering, take the prophets who spoke in the
name of the Lord. As you know, we consider
blessed those who have persevered ...*
James 5:10, 11

You are cutting your wisdom
teeth the first time you bite
off more than you can chew.

A FREE SPIRIT

... we have put our hope in the living God, who is the Savior of all men, and especially of those who believe.
1 Timothy 4:10

Letting go of your load will release a peace within you. This will allow your spirit to soar, to be free, to be completely given to God.

THE LIGHT OF GOD

This is the message we have heard from him and declare to you: God is light; in him there is no darkness at all.
1 John 1:5

God's love shines on us and brings music to our lives. And it is the light of God which lights up our lives in this dark world.

TO CARE ABOUT

*And we urge you, brothers ... encourage the
timid, help the weak, be patient with
everyone ... always try to be kind ...*
1 Thessalonians 5:14, 15

*L*etting Go
To let go is not to care
for, but to care about. To let go is
not to fix, but to be supportive. To
let go is not to judge, but to allow
another to be a human being. To let
go is not to be protective, it is to
permit another to face reality.

TRAGEDIES CAN BECOME TRIUMPHS

... "My soul glorifies the Lord and my spirit rejoices in God my Savior, for he has been mindful of the humble state of his servant ... "
Luke 1:46-48

How refreshing to know that healing does come to us, and tragedies can become triumphs. Songs which should be full of pain and anguish can reflect on God's perfect touch of comfort in our lives.

INDECISION

*... he who doubts is like a wave of
the sea, blown and tossed by the wind.*
James 1:6

Indecision can make life difficult ...
like the centipede that can't decide
which foot to put forward first.

MUSIC TO HEAVY HEARTS

And I will do whatever you ask in my name, so that the Son may bring glory to the Father.
John 14:13

It is easy to see bitterness creep in and a sense of frustration and futility grow because of wayward kids, a suicide, or other family death. It is then that we have to depend on the love of God to warm our heart. Remember: His love lights up our lives and brings music to our heavy hearts.

NOVEMBER 15

LET GOD TAKE OVER

*All the ways of the LORD are
loving and faithful for those who
keep the demands of his covenant.*
Psalm 25:10

Probably the very hardest thing you will
have to do for your own recovery, and
for the restoration of your relationship
with your child, is to let that child go!
Let him or her go and let God take over.

NOVEMBER 16

LONG-TERM INVESTMENTS

He who did not spare his own Son, but gave him up for us all — how will he not also, along with him, graciously give us all things?
Romans 8:32

Devastation in the family is not solved by a little Band-Aid. It takes major therapy and reconstructive surgery. Remember, children are not short-term notes but long-term investments.

SPECIAL ENOUGH

*"And we know that in all things God works
for the good of those who love him, who have
been called according to his purpose."*
Romans 8:28

It is easier to let go if we are
convinced that God cares about us,
and that He considers us special
enough to work things out to our
very best advantage (even if it
doesn't look like much at first).

NOVEMBER 18

THE WRONG TRACK

*Set your minds on things above,
not on earthly things.*
Colossians 3:2

If your train of thought isn't
getting you anywhere, you're
probably on the wrong track.

NOVEMBER 19

ALWAYS SPECIAL

For the LORD watches over the
way of the righteous, but the way
of the wicked will perish.
Psalm 1:6

I am special to God, even if it isn't
my birthday, or Mother's Day, or any
other holiday. God loves me every
day, and I am always special to Him.

NOVEMBER 20

A WHITE ROBE OF RIGHTEOUSNESS

He who overcomes will, like them, be dressed in white. I will never blot out his name from the book of life, but will acknowledge his name before my Father and his angels.
Revelation 3:5

Jesus has wiped the slate clean. He cannot see my sin because it is covered by His blood. Remember, He gave me a white robe of righteousness which is kept clean by a special detergent called forgiveness.

NOVEMBER 21

GIVE YOUR CHILD TO GOD

*He who fears the Lord has a secure fortress, and
for his children it will be a refuge.*
Proverbs 14:26

Confident in God's love and
acceptance, let go and let God
take your child. Give him to God!

LOVE MORE

*Trust in him at all times, O people; pour out
your hearts to him, for God is our refuge.*
Psalm 62:8

Letting Go

To let go is not to deny but to
accept. To let go is not to adjust
everything to my desires but to take
each day as it comes and to cherish the
moment. To let go is not to regret the
past but to grow and live for the future.
To let go is to fear less and love more.

GOD WILL UNDERTAKE

Save us and help us with your right hand,
that those you love may be delivered.
Psalm 60:5

You have given your prodigal to
God and have taken your hands off.
Now you are ready to ask God to do
whatever is necessary to bring that
child back to Him. We may see circumstances that tear us apart, but
God will undertake to reach the
rebel, often in very dramatic ways.

IN HIS ARMS

"The LORD brings death and makes alive; he brings down to the grave and raises up."
1 Samuel 2:6

The only time you have permission to take your child back is when Jesus drops him! When do you think that will be? Never! Then don't worry — Jesus has him in His arms, and you can't do nearly as well with your child as Jesus can.

IF WE REALLY TRUST GOD

We have come to share in Christ
if we hold firmly till the end
the confidence we had at first.
Hebrews 3:14

If we really trust God, then we won't fear anything. If we really trust God, then we can meet the challenges of life head on, knowing that in the end, God's side "wins".

HIS MASTER PLAN

"Surely God is my salvation; I will trust and not be afraid. The LORD, the LORD, is my strength and my song; he has become my salvation."
Isaiah 12:2

The trusting heart is the sharing heart. The trusting heart can look outside of its own predicament, see the plight of others, and offer help. The trusting heart is just waiting to be used by God for His master plan.

LET HIM TAKE ACTION

Jesus called out with a loud voice, "Father, into your hands I commit my spirit." When he had said this, he breathed his last.
Luke 23:46

It is our knowing and our caring that should compel us as parents to bring our rebellious children to the Lord, to lay them at His feet, and then to let Him take action on their behalf.

LET GO – AND LET GOD!

He will keep you strong to the end,
so that you will be blameless on the
day of our Lord Jesus Christ.
1 Corinthians 1:8

One of the surest evidences of faith in God is our being able to turn away from a difficult situation in which we have done our best, and to give our attention to other matters with a calm, untroubled mind. Let go – and let God!

TANGLES IN A YARN BALL

*For we are God's workmanship, created in
Christ Jesus to do good works, which God
prepared in advance for us to do.*
Ephesians 2:10

Did you ever think of your life, with
all the mistakes, sins, and woes of the
past, like tangles in a yarn ball, with
such a mess that you could never begin
to straighten it out? It is such a comfort to drop the tangles into God's
hands — and then leave them there.

RELEASE THE LOAD

*Blessed is the man who makes
the LORD his trust ...*
Psalm 40:4

If there is only one message I could get through to you this month, it would be to help you place your child in God's hands, and then release the load to Him.

DECEMBER

DECEMBER 1

THE INNER JOY

*Finally, brothers, whatever is true,
whatever is noble, whatever is right,
whatever is pure, whatever is lovely, whatever is
admirable – if anything is excellent or praiseworthy – think about such things.*
Philippians 4:8

*F*or this month, let's concentrate
on the inner joy we can have, and
set our grief aside for a little while.
We are growing, maturing, and
learning to live in the real world again.

DECEMBER 2

SURVIVING

It is because of him that you are in Christ Jesus, who has become for us wisdom from God – that is, our righteousness, holiness and redemption.
1 Corinthians 1:30, 31

When I get all the way to December, I feel as if I have really accomplished a lot. Just surviving is a big achievement!

DECEMBER 3

MICROWAVE MATURITY

But the fruit of the Spirit is love, joy, peace,
patience, kindness, goodness, faithfulness ...
Galatians 5:22

Remember the old saying, "I want
my patience, God, and I want it
now"? Well, there is no such thing
as microwave maturity. We get
maturity the hard way — we earn it.

DECEMBER 4

PATIENCE

Brothers, as an example of patience in the face of suffering, take the prophets who spoke in the name of the Lord.
James 5:10

I think the most comfort to people who have to be patient in their situation is this: "Patience is the ability to idle your motor when you feel like stripping your gears!"

DECEMBER 5

A REVERSAL PROCESS

Do not conform any longer to the pattern of this world, but be transformed by the renewing of your mind. Then you will be able to test and approve what God's will is – his good, pleasing and perfect will.
Romans 12:2

There is a reversal process which takes time, and we are all learning about patience. One helpful prayer called "reversal" goes like this: "Lord, for so long I thought Your love demanded that I change. At last, I am beginning to understand that Your love changed me!"

JUST AS I AM

*Therefore we do not lose heart. Though
outwardly we are wasting away, yet
inwardly we are being renewed day by day.*
2 Corinthians 4:16

God loves me so much that He will
accept me just as I am, but He loves
me too much to leave me that way!

YOUR PROGRESS

Commit your way to the LORD;
trust in him and he will do this ...
Psalm 37:5

*L*ook back over the last few months of your life. Can you see the progress you have made? Congratulate yourself on your progress, no matter how slight it might be. You are working on it, and trusting God, and that's all that counts.

A LITTLE TASTE OF WHOLENESS

… For the LORD is a God of justice.
Blessed are all who wait for him!
Isaiah 30:18

Often when we start to recover,
we slump back into a depression.
That's because we get a little taste
of wholeness, and then we don't
have the patience to wait for the
rest of the situation to be resolved.

DECEMBER 9

A DEADLINE

But we have this treasure in jars of clay to show that this all-surpassing power is from God and not from us.
2 Corinthians 4:7

Four Steps Out of Depression
1. Realize you are depressed.
2. Tell yourself this is not a permanent thing. It is passing.
3. Anything that is going to leave can be endured for a short time.
4. Set a deadline for it to end, and tell yourself you will allow your depression to last until a certain time – and then you will be rid of it.

DECEMBER 10

AT LAST

Do not be anxious about anything, but in everything, by prayer and petition, with thanksgiving, present your requests to God.
Philippians 4:6

*"**H**ope deferred makes the heart sick; but when dreams come true at last, there is life and joy."*
Proverbs 13:12 TLB

DECEMBER 11

GOLD IN THE MAKING

*But he knows the way that I take; when he
has tested me, I will come forth as gold.*
Job 23:10

Did you know that if all the gold in the
world were melted down into a solid
cube it would be about the size of an
eight-room house? If you had all that
gold, billions of dollars worth, you could
not buy a friend, character, peace of
mind, a clear conscience, or eternal life!
And yet, you are gold in the making
because of the trials you have come
through! Isn't that an exciting idea!

JOURNEY TO BECOMING WHOLE

*Therefore encourage one another and build
each other up, just as in fact you are doing.*
1 Thessalonians 5:11

I could share literally dozens of
letters with you from people who
are making progress on their journey
to becoming whole people again.
You are not alone. Take my word for
it, your black-pit days will pass,
and balance will return to your life.

DECEMBER 13

COMMON SUFFERING

And do not forget to do good and to share with others, for with such sacrifices God is pleased.
Hebrews 13:16

*T*hose of us who have rebellious prodigals can rejoice with each other at our successes, and cry with each other when things go wrong. We are bound together because of the special grief we have had, and our common suffering is a far greater link than common joy.

DECEMBER 14

CONTINUE ON

*Now may the Lord of peace himself
give you peace at all times and in
every way. The Lord be with all of you.*
2 Thessalonians 3:16

Learn how to lay down
your agonies, pick up your
credentials, and continue on.

SOFTENING THE BLOWS

*Therefore, as God's chosen people, holy and
dearly loved, clothe yourselves with compassion,
kindness, humility, gentleness and patience.*
Colossians 3:12

It is a long trip for most of us,
but we can help each other on the
journey by loving, caring, sharing,
and softening the blows of life.

DECEMBER 16

GOD'S FAMILY

*For this reason I kneel before the Father
from whom his whole family in heaven
and on earth derives its name.*
Ephesians 3:14

We are on the same trip. Some are
farther along, and some are behind you,
but we are all on the same road. Let's
arrive and be claimed by the Lord as
part of His family. We'll have plenty of
time to get really close in heaven. There
is no unclaimed freight in God's family!

DECEMBER 17

FAST DAYS

*We want each of you to show this
same diligence to the very end, in
order to make your hope sure.*
Hebrews 6:11

*B*ecause of the fast days in which we
live, we are used to fast food, rapid
transit, microwave ovens, and instant
breakfasts. But instant emotional
maturity? There ain't no such thing!

DECEMBER 18

NOT ALONE

Answer me when I call to you, O my righteous God. Give me relief from my distress; be merciful to me and hear my prayer.
Psalm 4:2

You are not alone. There are thousands of us who have felt as you do now, who hurt as you are hurting, and we are making it. We are survivors, and you will be, too. Just find comfort in knowing that you are not by yourself.

A PROCESS

But solid food is for the mature,
who by constant use have trained
themselves to distinguish good from evil.
Hebrews 5:14

Maturity is a process. Over the long
haul, you can see a softening, a smooth-
ing out of the rough edges, a sensitivity
to God's working in our lives, a lessen-
ing of the pain we have experienced
and even inflicted on ourselves.

COAXING A HABIT

*Anyone, then, who knows the good he
ought to do and doesn't do it, sins.*
James 4:17

You cannot toss a habit out the
window. It must be coaxed down
the stairs one step at a time.

GENTLE HEAVENLY ERASER

*The Lord is not slow in keeping his promise,
as some understand slowness. He is patient with
you, not wanting anyone to perish,
but everyone to come to repentance.*
2 Peter 3:9

Someone once told me that God has a gentle heavenly eraser. It erases slowly sometimes, but it leaves no trace and it doesn't tear the paper. That's better than a fast swipe that tears as it erases.

THE CHOICEST COUNSELORS

*If we are distressed, it is for your comfort and
salvation; if we are comforted, it is for your
comfort, which produces in you patient endurance of the same sufferings we suffer.*
2 Corinthians 1:6

Remember: You who have endured
the stinging experiences are the
choicest counselors God can use.

COMPLETELY OUT

But the fruit of the Spirit is love, joy,
peace, patience, kindness, goodness,
faithfulness, gentleness and self-control ...
Galatians 5:22, 23

Shopping List
All of a sudden I've noticed that I'm
completely out of generosity – I must
look for some more. And I mustn't
forget to look for some tolerance; it's a
good substitute when you're low on
indulgence. And the last time I was
shopping I saw some interesting samples
of kindness I want to look at again. Oh,
I almost forgot – I must try to match
some patience, too. I saw some on a friend
yesterday, and it was very becoming.

INCREASING MATURITY

(W)ho through faith are shielded by God's power until the coming of the salvation that is ready to be revealed in the last time.
1 Peter 1:5

When you go forth to recover after your year of molding, know that your maturity will keep increasing every day of your life, even when you don't feel that God is doing anything with you.

GOD IS IN CHARGE

... your eyes saw my unformed body. All the days ordained for me were written in your book before one of them came to be.
Psalm 139:16

As we wind down our year's journey, I want to remind you again that God is in charge. From a seemingly useless lump of clay, He can fashion something beautiful and useful.

DECEMBER 26

GOD'S MILL

*We have come to share in Christ if
we hold firmly till the end the
confidence we had at first.*
Hebrews 3:14

*G*od's mill grinds slowly
but exceedingly fine.

DECEMBER 27

INNER HEALING

Therefore, as God's chosen people, holy and dearly loved, clothe yourselves with compassion, kindness, humility, gentleness and patience.
Colossians 3:12

Go on loving your child, and then reach out to others around you who are hurting. This will lessen your heartache, and by reaching outward, you will find much inner healing flowing back into you.

NEVER FORSAKEN

*When Christ, who is your life, appears, then
you also will appear with him in glory.*
Colossians 3:4

*H*e didn't bring you this far to leave you.
He didn't teach you to swim to
let you drown. He didn't build His
home in you to move away. He
didn't lift you up to let you down.

DECEMBER 29

ONE'S STOCK OF GOODNESS

It is God's will that you should be sanctified ...
1 Thessalonians 4:3

*S*hopping List
I must remember to get my sense
of humor mended, and keep my
eyes open for some goodness – it's
surprising how quickly one's stock
of goodness becomes depleted.
It would be a good day for me to check
to see if there is a special being offered
on charity, optimism, and love – things a
person should never risk running out of.

BECOME A TREASURE

So then, those who suffer according to God's
will should commit themselves to their
faithful Creator and continue to do good.
1 Peter 4:19

God is in control, and maturity
will come in His time — not yours —
both to you and your child. Be
patient, be faithful, and become a
treasure in His eternal kingdom.

TOWARD THE GOAL

Do not conform any longer to the pattern of this world, but be transformed by the renewing of your mind. Then you will be able to test and approve what God's will is ...
Romans 12:2

Don't let the world around you squeeze you into its own mold, but let God remold your minds from within, so that you may prove in practice that the plan of God for you is good, meets all his demands and moves toward the goal of true maturity. Romans 12:2 PHILLIPS